BEAUTY REINVENTED

*How to **EMBRACE GRAY HAIR**,*
***UPGRADE** Your Self-Confidence*
*and **REDEFINE** Your Beauty*

NIKOL JOHNSON

Table of Contents

ABOUT THE BOOK

GOING GRAY IN YOUR THIRTIES IS NOT EASY. It's not what society says is *right* or *OK*. I want to share my journey with women all over the world and let you know by example that it is *OK* to be your authentic self, no matter what society says.

I cannot tell you how many women come up to me, write on my social media outlets, and tell me that they could never go gray because it just wouldn't "look good" on them. How can you say this without *actually going gray?* It's like saying, "Ohhh that ice cream you are eating looks amazing... I am practically drooling just looking at it... but I know I wouldn't like it."

It's time to break the rules, ladies, and embrace your authentic self! It's time that we stop making excuses, stop being insecure, and stop buying into the advertisements, glossy magazines, and commercials that only show women with colored hair.

In this book, I will show you how to conquer your fear of the unknown and taboo world of going gray. I will help you build self-confidence so you can *stand out* in a crowd and embrace your authentic self. You will be one strong, *fierce,* bold woman ready to welcome your gorgeous gray once you finish this book!

I know you are on board and ready to rock your new image or you wouldn't have picked this up. I will hold your hand through all of the emotional ups and downs because I have been there. I will give you the strength to keep moving forward when you are down and feeling "frumpy and old." I will pick you up and make you feel alive and beautiful again.

Packed with self-assessments, humor, and grit, I will share expert beauty secrets that will help you with your transition into new makeup color palettes. I'll give you the best skin care tips to keep your skin looking hydrated, young, and glowing. I will help you feel that *you are not alone* by sharing interviews with real women that have gone gray; relating what their experience has been, and offering great advice for you in your gray hair journey.

This book is also a bit of a workbook, so if you are reading the eBook version, be sure to have a pad of paper beside you, or a notepad available on your computer. If you are reading the book in paper form, space has been provided to write your answers.

Sit back, get comfortable, and *celebrate yourself* with one of my signature cocktails at the beginning of each chapter.

Gray hair is not an easy journey, but I am here for you every step of the way. I will offer encouraging, practical advice that will allow you to push through the bumps in the uncomfortable gray road ahead.

Are you ready to say YES to your gray hair journey? Well then, ladies, *Let's Get This Beauty Started!*

ABOUT THE AUTHOR

On-Air beauty expert, entrepreneur, licensed Esthetician, and founder of *Fresh Beauty Studio* and *Beauty Reinvented* Nikol Johnson rocked the beauty world when she decided to liberate her gray hair at thirty-nine. Breaking the beauty rules for Nikol came with a little hesitation. In the world of beauty where being young and wrinkle free is Queen, how would the world react to a woman willingly letting her hair go gray and just turning forty? Working as a FORD model since the age of fifteen and being told by the industry to be everything but herself, Nikol eventually decided to *own her beauty* and let the gray out.

Before her gray hair journey, Nikol launched *Fresh Beauty Studio* in 2006 and has spent the past twelve years creating gorgeous faces at her boutique makeup studio in South Florida. There she concentrates on advanced permanent makeup techniques, airbrush makeup, and flawless skin, giving hundreds of women confidence and style through beauty and education.

Runner-up in 2016 *People Magazine Natural Beauty Search,* Nikol knew she was on to something big with helping women embrace their unique gray hair journey and beauty. One of Nikol's fastest growing videos is *her Gray Hair Journey* with over 200K views. As a niche social influencer, Nikol has over 3 million views on her beauty YouTube channel. She reaches tens of thousands of women across her social media platforms who are looking for a change in the anti-aging beauty industry.

MESSAGE FROM NIKOL

I AM INSPIRED BY YOU

TO ALL THE WOMEN THAT ARE ON THE
CUSP OF CHANGE, LEAN IN AND
EMBRACE YOUR POWER.

THIS ONE'S FOR YOU, LADIES.

INTRODUCTION:

What Is
Beauty Reinvented?

WHY WRITE A BOOK ABOUT GRAY HAIR? Being a writer was always in the back of my mind since my high school composition class days, but I never felt a deep desire to write on any particular subject until I went through infertility in 2014. I was like a bird without wings; trying to navigate the IVF game or should I say moneymaking industry? I felt that women should get the raw heads-up from a girl who went through nine IVF procedures before they jumped with two ovaries into their own messy and confusing life of infertility. Soon, however, I realized it wasn't my infertility journey I should be writing about.

I started writing a beauty blog at a time when saying the word *blog* made people say, "bless you." Not many people knew what a blog was back in 2007, but I did. I couldn't wait to write and share all my knowledge of makeup, beauty, and skin care. Fast forward to 2014 when I created a second blog dedicated to my IVF life with a beauty and fashion edge called "Not Just a Beauty Blogger." I wanted to infuse my beauty and fashion background into an area of life that was not very colorful, glamorous, or fun. I needed an immediate outlet for what I was going through with IVF. I wanted to share how I was getting through a life experience that wasn't expected and also completely devastating.

At the time, there were only a handful of women sharing their infertility journeys on YouTube. Most of these infertility channels were depressing and dark. I knew that I wasn't being authentic with my beauty videos; pretending that my personal life wasn't affecting my beauty channel and blog. I couldn't keep up with my production schedule and I knew it was time to allow my viewers to know what was going on with me.

I started writing about my infertility experience and found that it wasn't enough; so I created a YouTube channel to document my life *vlog-style* through doctor's appointments, self-inflicting hormone injections, and traveling back and forth to Colorado. I wore nail polish with names like "Fierce No Fear" and bold, bright lipsticks that kept me going with positive mantras. I wanted to give strength to women who felt like giving up. In retrospect, I may have over shared aspects of my journey, but I was fueled by anger, no answers, being just a number, and the determination to get pregnant.

I didn't think much about the fact that I had never shared anything personal publicly on my beauty YouTube channel or blog. By putting my journey and life out there in such a public way, I found my tribe of women. Women came out of the social media darkness and revealed themselves to me. They could relate to me now that I showed my hot messy life and not a beautiful makeup tutorial. I was real and raw; allowing one of the most vulnerable life experiences to unfold through social media (something that is very uncommon in the beautiful world of beauty). I started to feel not so alone or isolated, finally feeling that perhaps I wasn't the only one going through such a dark moment.

During this period of struggle, I was on my fourth IVF cycle, and my gray hair exploded. Doctors will tell you that my gray hair has nothing to do with stress, IVF, and synthetic hormones, but I believe differently.

You can imagine how I felt walking into a fertility clinic with massive white roots and black hair. Talk about feeling out of place! It wasn't unusual to have all the women in the waiting area stop and look up from their magazines when I entered the room. I would see pairs of eyes peeking out over the top of the magazine pages with a look of horror. I would make up all kinds of thoughts about what these girls were thinking; like *"Holy Lord, I hope that's not from IVF." "Please, please, please tell me that I am not going to go gray like that." "Girl, this is a fertility clinic, not an assisted living facility."* A time I don't want to revisit.

I put my body through an enormous amount of pressure from two IUI's, five IVF cycles, two fresh embryo transfers, two frozen transfers, PGS testing, hormones, sadness, stress, anxiety, loneliness, and multiple surgeries all in a matter of four years. In the end, I was left holding the bag of failure. On top of all of this, my hair was going gray? How could this be happening? I already have this ridiculous label from my doctor's ancient medical books telling me I have "advanced maternal aging" which I shot back each time with "Let's get with the time dude and um don't mind my gray hair." My anger not only came from my bold and fierce Greek roots but from constantly fighting to find answers and not be stamped with a diagnosis of "unexplained infertility" (which from my research is not a real diagnosis). I finally proved my "Unexplained" with a diagnosis of stage-three endometriosis after going through a two-hour surgery.

Enter my gray hair journey.

I was at the point emotionally where I didn't care. I didn't care that I put my Frenchie in a doggie carriage and strolled her right into the fertility clinic to the front desk and checked in. That's right; this is me all gray and crazy, and YES this is my *doghter* in a stroller. What? Is that weird? I didn't care that I got the 10% senior discount at TJ Maxx on Monday; I was finished caring what society thought of infertility and gray hair. I thought *Who goes through two taboo experiences at one time? Maybe this is good luck?*

I did have one of my clients (an Indian Bride) tell me that in her culture it was terrible luck to cover up my gray stripe. At this point, it wasn't important that I had black and white hair at thirty-eight; I was tired of the nonsense and wasn't about to fight my entire head turning gray.

So, on my fortieth birthday, I decided to stop dyeing, rock the gray hair, and empower women all over the world to embrace their authentic self, break the social beauty rules, and redefine their lives.

Welcome to *Beauty Reinvented.*

DRINK: NIK-TINI

1.5 oz Patron Silver Tequila

1oz Cointreau

.5 oz Fresh lime juice

1 dash Cranberry juice

Garnish: Lime wedge

Glass: Martini

Here I Am

JUNE 12, 1992 WAS ONE OF THE MOST INCREDIBLE DAYS of my life, and also the most intense. I remember driving down in the car to Aventura Mall in Miami listening to Seal and singing along with my Mom. I wasn't nervous, which is surprising considering what was on the line that day.

Mom and I parked and walked into the mall, the cold rush of crisp air blowing back my long hair when the sliding doors opened. We weren't sure where we were supposed to go but soon found the giant stage with the words "Supermodel of America Contest" written above the platform.

I looked around at all the chairs that were being set up, and it started to sink in. The modeling contest was happening, and it was happening to me. I had entered a modeling contest sponsored by FORD Models, Ultima II Cosmetics and JC Penney. Even though I didn't think I had a chance, I took a chance and entered it anyway.

And now - here I was. Because I was picked as a semi-finalist in the local contest, I was now competing against twenty other hopeful models for a chance to go to New York City, compete at a

national level on the *Maury Povich Show,* and get a
modeling contract with FORD Models.

The day was a blur of sweaty palms and heart
palpitations. After I heard my name called to enter
stage left, I walked out in front of hundreds of
people, clapping and cheering. It was a mock photo
shoot, and here I was — completely unsure of myself
— posing for strangers and the judges. I had to tell
myself *don't fall off the stage!*

I loved the excitement and high that being on stage
gave me. It was both a terrifying and exhilarating
feeling that would follow me my entire modeling
career and life, for better or for worse.

When my name was called as the winner, and one
of the judges handed me a bouquet of red roses, I
had no idea what to think or do. I was almost
embarrassed by all the attention. ME? Did I win? I
kept thinking *what did I do to deserve this?*

Even though I was truly excited about it, I kept my
modeling career a secret. I already had some minor
issues with girls at school and didn't want to fuel any
more jealousy by telling everyone I was modeling. I
mean, announcing that you are a model at fifteen is
never greeted with tears of joy, with other teenage
girls being happy for you! So this secret became an
underlining thread in my career.

One of the perks of winning the Supermodel of
America contest was the trunk of makeup I received
from Ultima II Cosmetics. Mom always teased me
that the haul of makeup up for grabs was the reason
I wanted to enter the contest, and deep down, I
knew she was right.

High school wasn't easy for me. Yes, I got decent
grades, and was on the cheerleading squad and
even made co-captain my freshman year. I got
involved in a lot of activities and dated the star
football player, but an incredible feeling of distrust
of other people always hung over me. I felt like I
couldn't let anyone see who I was. I couldn't be just

me; I always protected myself and never let anyone get to know who I was.

I felt like I just didn't fit in and had rules for myself that were very rigid. For example, *I always called my parents and told them where I was no matter what time it was.... I was the designated driver when everyone went out because I wouldn't drink before I was twenty-one and everyone else was drinking... I felt like I had to be in control at all times...* The list goes on and on. You get the idea; I was extremely tough on myself and had unrealistic expectations of needing to be perfect.

Because of this fear of letting anyone get too close, I ended up having superficial, surface relationships all throughout high school, college, and beyond. I didn't want anyone to know I had won this super cool contest and wasn't quite sure how I would keep my classmates from knowing I would be on national television in just a few short weeks.

Going to New York City was the highlight of my year in 1992. I received an all-expenses-paid trip to the city, complete with a first-class agenda including a professional photo shoot with a New York photographer; meeting Eileen and Jerry Ford, the owners of FORD models; five-star dinners; lux hotel accommodations; and being around the who's who in the fashion business.

Word got out that I was on the Maury Povich show. I didn't win that contest, but I did walk away with a modeling contract with FORD Models. From that moment on, my life would be completely different.

I went through two decades of my life being told how to look, how much I should weigh on a scale, how I should wear my makeup, and even what athletic activities I could enjoy. There would be no rollerblading, no skiing, and no laying out in the sun. I had curfews, diet restrictions, and an unnatural world.

I want you to know and understand that even though I was a "model" I struggled like everyone else to be accepted, to be loved, and to fight my negative thoughts. Because I was such a people-pleaser, I just went along with what people wanted and expected of me. I wanted to appear perfect; pulled together and flawless.

I soon realized that I had spun my life into a tight little ball of emotion that never allowed me to feel or be felt. I protected myself from relationships, people, and even friends, all in the name of fear and insecurity.

In 2011 I reconnected with the man who would become my husband. (Fun fact: We went to high school together! He likes to tell everyone that I was in love with him back then, but in reality, with me being a lowly freshman and him a lofty senior, we rarely mingled except for football games when I was cheering him on when he was on the field showing his Big Play football skills!) When we started to date, he told me I had anxiety and should see a professional.

You can imagine how that went over! I think I broke up with him because of that statement, which shows you how profoundly protected and unaware of myself I was. The anxiety that I thought I didn't have was OFF the charts.

No matter who you are, everyone has something they are working through. For me, it was a touch of OCD, anxiety, and fear. I used to keep creating websites, products, content, videos; you name it, to keep my mind off of the real issues. I would pack my schedule until there was never one second of down-time until... ...

I hit a wall with infertility in 2014. I was clueless as to how people perceived me and how I came across to others. My diagnosis of "Unexplained Infertility" humbled me and I finally became real with myself. I was stripped of all the glamour and the excitement of the life I knew, and instead spent 90% of my time in stirrups; listening to doctors count my follicles.

I don't think I would have accepted my gray hair if I had not gone through my infertility journey. I discovered my true self when the chips were down, and I was tired of trying to live up to all these ideas that were formed in my head since I was a little girl. Finally, I was ready to take on society's perception of women aging and hair. I wanted to lift women up and leave this life knowing I gave my whole heart and soul to inspire, encourage, and ignite the Silver Linings we all have inside us.

You determine your silver lining. YOU decide if you want to see it or not. I have chosen to gloss the world with my bold gray attitude, and I hope you will join me!

SILVER LININGS

from this chapter

_____

_____

_____

_____

_____

_____

_____

DRINK: NO RULES

2 oz Grey Goose Vodka

1 oz dry vermouth

Shaken not stirred

Garnish: 3 olives on a silver toothpick

2

Breaking
the Beauty Rules
(3 RULES TO BREAK NOW)

HOW MANY TIMES HAVE YOU BEEN TOLD, *No you can't wear that eyeshadow with that lipstick* or *you have to match your outfit color to your bag and shoes?* Who makes up these beauty rules? The strange thing is, 99% of women will follow them without questioning why this rule even exists! Same goes for gray hair. Who says that gray hair makes you old? Seriously, I want you to think about this question for a minute. Why do we believe gray hair makes us old when the majority of the population is gray by forty-five or at least somewhat gray? Take away the ability to dye your hair, and I think you would be shocked to see how many women are gray!

I remember playing the game *Old Maid* when I was little. From a very young age, we have been brainwashed that *gray hair* translates to being *old*.

Not just *old* but also *frumpy* and *unattractive*. We relate *blue plate special* with gray hair, and the phrase *senior citizen* produces visuals of women with gray hair. In fact, society has created a unique dialect for gray-haired women by calling them Silvers, senior citizens, and the elderly, like it is an exclusive old club.

What if we flip the switch on the meaning of gray hair? *Bold, Fierce, Empowered, Authentic* are the new words that we will use in this book to describe and represent women that have chosen to *stop* dyeing their hair and embrace naturally gorgeous gray, white, or silver hair.

Allure Magazine published an article in January 2018 that stated, "Gray Hair is Set to Be 2018's Most Popular Hair Color Trend." Is gray hair a trend or is it a reality? If you ask the twenty-something girls dyeing their hair gray if it is a trend, they will likely tell you that it is. However, if you ask a forty-year-old woman why she *stopped* dyeing her hair, she will tell you it's not a trend but a bold, redefining life decision.

Gray hair is a very personal choice. I am not saying gray hair is for everyone, nor am I shaming women that want to dye their hair until their very last day on earth. The gray hair movement is about independence, learning about yourself, and expressing your authentic beauty. There is pushback from society, women, friends, husbands, partners, etc. when you decide to go gray because it's still very taboo. I never understood why you had to hide your age. Is it shameful to be living and celebrating a new year? We have one life to live! Let's start celebrating every part of ourselves with joy and gratitude.

BEAUTY RULE TO BREAK #1:

YOU DON'T HAVE TO LOOK LIKE EVERYONE ELSE

Social media has become the enemy when it comes to self-image, confidence, and comparing ourselves to everyone else. How many times have you said to yourself *I am just going to "look" at Instagram...* Down the rabbit hole you go, spending hours scrolling through filtered pictures that eventually leave you feeling drained, overwhelmed, and not good enough. **I have been there,** and it is a total compare and despair. To embrace yourself and build confidence let's start with a social media break-up. Don't freak — I am not saying forever — but just enough time to regroup. To *refocus* your energy on yourself and what is important to you in your life, taking a break from social media is a *must*.

Ladies, it's not normal to see picture after picture of enhanced faces, perfect skin, and six-pack abs. You are looking at an altered world expecting to look into the mirror and see perfection, but it just doesn't exist! Don't set yourself up for failure; take what I like to call a "Social glam nap" from all the social outlets and watch your self-confidence soar.

What does taking a break look like for you? Is it one day, one week or a month? Decide what you feel will enhance your life and fill the time you used to spend scrolling and comparing with family, reading a great book (like this one!), taking a walk with your dog, or just reconnecting with yourself. When you step away from the noise and focus on YOU and no one else, you will gain more clarity and experience less stress.

Breaking Beauty challenge: I want you to pick one feature on your face that you like, and write it down here.

We will come back to this later.

BEAUTY RULE TO BREAK #2:

CHECKING IN ON NEGATIVE SELF-TALK

How many times have you looked in the mirror and said something negative to yourself about your face, body, or skin; or someone gave you a compliment on your lipstick color, hair, or outfit; only for you to dismiss their positive comment with a negative? **We all do,** but we need to start a *positive* mental dialog within ourselves. Even *one* negative comment swirling around in your brain can ruin your entire energy for the day. Check in with yourself and see what you are saying to yourself in your head on a daily basis. Do you repeat negative comments people have said to you in the past? Do you pass a reflective window on your way to work and think, *Ugh, I look so fat...?*

Now more than ever we are bombarded with the pressure to look like we are not aging. Women are under more and more pressure to be wrinkle free, pulled together at every moment, and to do it all. The biggest mistake you can make is trying to be something you are not or trying to look like someone else! If we are going to change what society thinks about aging, it starts with ourselves. We need to break out of the mold that we think we need to be in and show the world what beautiful women look like at every age.

I have had many battles with myself about keeping a positive outlook on my changing beauty. I would see myself in the mirror and think *OMG is that my hair it's so white is that me?* Then all the negative comments would start flooding in. It would put me in such a bad mood that I started writing positive words on Post-It notes and sticking them all over the house. Post-Its are a great little trick to keep you focused on what is essential and what is beautiful and different about your unique beauty.

Ladies, you will have bad days where you feel completely drained and not beautiful at all, and that's OK. It's not about being this positive Girl Boss all day every day! It's about recognizing the areas where you bring yourself down, that tear at the vulnerable areas of your physical self and dull out your sparkle. There are plenty of people that will do that for you, but *don't be one of them.*

Living your authentic self looks very different for each and every woman out there. It doesn't just mean going dye-free; it means letting your true self develop and not being afraid to show the world who you are.

I think that it's easy to hide what you truly feel and want to be because of the fear that you won't be accepted. This is how I felt going gray in my thirties! I thought I was the odd woman out walking into a room. I felt like something was *wrong* with me because I just couldn't bring myself to dye my hair that fake black anymore. It was almost like I hit the fast-forward button on aging and had a choice to make: either I was *in* or I was *out* but I couldn't be *both.*

What negative comments do you tend to say to yourself on an hourly, daily, or weekly basis? How does that make you feel?

_____

_____

_____

Write down the one thing you say to yourself that you want to break free from.

_____

_____

_____

Now replace it with a positive statement that you will say to yourself each morning.

_____

_____

_____

BEAUTY RULE TO BREAK #3:

BREAKING THE MOLD & CREATING YOUR OWN UNIQUE BEAUTY PATH

It's incredible to me to see how many women on social media are just copying each other. Take a prominent fashion blogger, for example. She stages and takes a picture overhead of flowers, a wallet, designer tennis shoes, and sunglasses. Oh, don't forget the Starbucks coffee cup all cramped together in her car literally on top of the gearshift, which looks so bizarre and unnatural. Then you have fifty other fashion bloggers doing the same thing.

Contrived? Yes. Interesting? No. It's the *copycat syndrome,* and you don't need the "It" beauty product that every beauty blogger is showing you.

Social Media is where you can get overwhelmed by the number of choices in the makeup and skin care world. Your beauty needs to be set apart and work for *you.* Magazines, TV, commercials, and blogs will show you the "trending" products that you have to use (mostly on Instagram these are paid or sponsored posts by influencers) but you, my dear, need to create your beauty path by finding the right products that work for you; not just those that are trending.

DON'T FOLLOW BEAUTY, BE BEAUTY

What does creating your beauty path look like for you? It's not as hard as it sounds. Every woman should have a simple but effective skin care routine she feels comfortable using every morning and night. You don't need hundreds of products; you only need three to four products to create beautiful skin, but you will have to experiment with the right formulations for your skin type. (We will talk more about this in Chapter 8.) Do you have naturally curly hair? Stop straightening it and let it be curly!

I recently had one of my regular clients walk into the studio, and she had these gorgeous tight curls. She seemed a little uncomfortable — almost like I wouldn't approve — and uncertain of herself until I said, "Oh my gosh, your hair is so beautiful!" I had never seen her hair curly. It never dawned on me that she had been straightening her hair all this time! I told her I thought her hair looked *gorgeous* and you could see she just *radiated* with her naturally curly hair.

SILVER SISTER SPOTLIGHT

RHIANNON GARDIER

Rhiannon is a Licensed Esthetician and Cosmetic Laser Technician who decided to stay at home for a while to focus on her kids and her health. Rhiannon will be celebrating her 15th wedding anniversary this year and is very excited about this milestone. Her husband's support through her gray hair journey means the world to her. Rhiannon posts YouTube videos of her documented gray hair transition. She recently created an Instagram account to continue inspiring others as well as encouraging herself.

Rhiannon's followers love the fact that she's not only growing her gray out, but that she is also a naturally curly girl. There is a demographic of women out there who are looking for ladies embracing both silver hair and curls, hence the title of her channel: *Silver Curl Journey.* Rhiannon hopes to be an example to her daughter, showing her that gray hair is ageless and beautiful.

Q: When did you start seeing gray hair and what were your initial thoughts?

I remember the day I found my first gray hair. I was about 16-years-old, and at the time, I thought it was a rare strand of platinum blonde hair because it had no color. I actually plucked it right out of my head, twirled it into a circle and saved it in a velvet ring box. A few months later, I discovered another one of those colorless hairs in my head. That's when I realized, "Oh wow. I'm getting gray hair already??"

Q: Did you have support from friends and family with your gray transition?

Oh yes. My husband had been encouraging me to grow out my naturally gray hair for at least a decade. Every time I had a baby, my gray hair would become more intense. He thought it was awesome, but I was having too much fun playing with vibrant highlights and fun box colors just to stop and be natural. When I finally decided to grow it out he was ecstatic.

Q: As a young mom, do you find other mothers celebrating your decision to go gray?

You know, it's hard to tell. Some of the questions I was getting, in the beginning, seemed very superficial. People thought I was going through a phase. They would ask how long I planned on growing it, whether I liked it or not, etc. It wasn't until very recently that I finally started receiving what I recognize to be genuine compliments.

Q: You have some very hip and trendy gray hairstyles from braids to super sleek. Tell us about your personal style.

Oh, thank you! I try to be creative because I do become bored very quickly with my hair. Hence the reason I played with hair color for 20 years. My style is more about simplicity than anything else. My kids have hectic schedules, which means I am always on the go. So whatever I can do in 10 minutes or less is my goal. I hardly ever wear makeup, but when I do, it only takes me a few minutes to apply it. You won't catch this girl contouring and 'baking' her foundation! Ha! I have naturally curly hair, so the easiest thing for me to do is a wash-and-go style. I have no shame in rocking ponytails (synthetic ones are fun!), pigtails, baseball caps, or bandanas on days when I'm in a rush. In fact, I seem to get more compliments when I have my hair pulled all the way back, exposing the majority of my silver hair. That's when braids come in handy. I braid my hair when I feel like I want a little attention. Haha!

Q: What advice would you give other women going through the first six months of not dyeing their hair?

Those first six months are the most eye-opening months for both yourself and the people around you. When you own it with cheerful confidence, everybody recognizes that as a type of beauty you didn't even know exists, even if you look in the mirror and don't see the beauty in yourself just yet. Your hair changing on the outside is kind of like that cocoon wrapping around that beautiful butterfly just waiting to be revealed. So hang in there! Once your transition is complete, you will feel like a new kind of beautiful. You will flutter around and attract all types of new people and adventures. I mean, look at me! I'm just a regular person who wanted to embrace her natural hair, and here I am being featured on the website of the very person whose videos inspired me to make this decision in the first place!

Q: Working with curly hair, can you tell us what hair products you currently use and recommend?

Sure! I use sulfate-free, silicone-free products. My current favorite brand is Cantu. I've tried a couple of others, but my hair texture and curl pattern didn't agree with them as much as they agree with Cantu.

If I could sample every curly girl product out there, I would! I just haven't had the chance to experiment some more.

I recommend trying anything and everything until you find what works for you. Some curls do well with silicones and a little sulfate. I don't believe in a one-size-fits-all method for curls. However, for those with curly silver hair, it is an absolute MUST to avoid too much heat (flat irons, etc.) and to use colorless products. Any cream or oil tinted with even the slightest shade of brown or yellow will stain our lovely white strands and dull the overall appearance of our hair. When and if that happens, there are plenty of purple shampoos that will help correct it.

Time's up! Are You *In* or *Out* with your gray hair journey? I want you to feel so confident with your decision that not one bad hair day (grab your Gray Attitude hat) or negative comment will change your fierce determination on where you are going with your personal gray hair journey. Rock on, my powerful silver sister, this is a very special time that you will always remember.

To connect with Rhiannon Gardier go to:

Instagram: @Silver30s
YouTube: Rhiannon Gardier

SILVER LININGS

from this chapter

_____

_____

_____

_____

_____

_____

_____

_____

_____

_____

_____

_____

_____

_____

_____

DRINK: SILVER STORM

2 oz Spiced Rum

Splash fresh lime juice

2 dashes Angostura bitters

Ginger Beer

Garnish 1 lime wedge

Glass: Highball

Pretty
Little Mess

IT'S AMAZING THE REACTION THE ENTIRE WORLD seems to have when a woman decides to go gray. I started thinking about the way we age. One day I didn't have a freckle, mole, or hyperpigmentation spot, and then all of a sudden, I did. Slowly I seemed to have a *lot* of beauty issues, but the world didn't take notice of my changing skin... so why does gray hair ignite such strong feelings and attention?

One day, I was complaining to my husband about how white my hair was in the front yet the back of my head was still so dark. He was like, "You know, it's kind of like geriatric in the front and party in the back." You can imagine my expression of disapproval. I immediately told him, "We are not talking for a very long time!" You have to have a sense of humor when going gray and not take everything so seriously. That one quote from him always makes me laugh out loud and puts a smile on my face.

Do you feel like a *pretty little mess* going gray? Well, honey, you are not alone! Gray hair is just a color, a loss of pigment; a tiny factor in the big scheme of things. We are all aging! Some are aging faster than others, but at the end of the day, Gray is Powerful. I lost count of how many people have come up to me and asked if my hair was natural! I know, completely crazy, because when I first was going gray, I thought, *Who would ever do this to themselves on purpose?* I remember thinking with the first dozen inquiring minds, *Did you color your hair gray? That would be NO! I would never have dyed my hair this color! Are you nuts?*

Wait, was I apologizing for my gray? Was I *ashamed* of my gray? Was I trying to *fit* into society's Beauty Rules? Yes, I was, and I decided right then, darling, that I needed to change my relationship with my gray hair.

You will go through many days where you question your decision to let your natural gorgeous gray go-to shine brightly on the world, to *represent* you. It's an incredible journey; a journey that many opt not to experience. Gray hair will teach you things about yourself that you never knew existed. Gray hair will help you conquer your fears and allow your personality to be bold and fierce.

Society has put too much pressure on women about aging. Of course, we all want to look our best, and I am not opposed to Botox, fillers or plastic surgery if you feel that is right for you. Just because you decided to go gray doesn't mean you have to turn down anti-aging treatments or procedures.

Are you surprised by my view on these topics? Remember, there are no rules I follow when it comes to my beauty. I don't let society, peers, or strangers dictate who I am or what I feel is right for my face; and neither should you. If you feel like you want to explore the world of Botox, that is a personal decision for *you* to decide, not for your husband, best friend or mother to choose for you. Stand up for your beauty; listen to yourself and what feels right to you.

I want to tell you a story on why I decided to start Botox at thirty years old. I have had women leave comments on my social media shaming me for doing Botox; saying that I am *not authentic* and I am *selling out*. The funny thing about these comments is I have never made an announcement that I even do Botox. I noticed a small cyst at the beginning of my left eyebrow around the age of twelve years old. I thought it was a strange area for a cyst to form but didn't think anything of it. Over the years, my cyst started to grow. I started setting up consults with plastic surgeons and ocular surgeons to get opinions on what my options were. I went to a total of eight consults because every doctor I would see gave me a different answer. One stated he would have to take my forehead down to get it out, and then the next doctor said it wasn't a big deal it would just pop out. Hold on a second; how could I have two drastically different opinions dealing with the same issue? The ocular surgeon said to wait until I had more wrinkles to conceal the scar, while another specialist had me do two MRI's to make sure it wasn't connected to the bone or brain. Geez, my little cyst that now is a hot mess minus the pretty is not as simple as I thought it would be to take out!

In 2003 I finally found a plastic surgeon that agreed to do the surgery, only to be told on my next visit that it was too dangerous to remove given the area the cyst was in on my face. So, my surgery was now off the table. I asked the doctor, "Since no one feels comfortable taking on my case, can I do Botox to lessen the heaviness and the line in front of the cyst?" He agreed (not that I thought he wouldn't).

Botox made me feel better about my issue. It smoothed out the bulge, and the cyst wasn't as noticeable. You might not have seen my cyst (or maybe you did notice it in my photographs or on my videos), but I do Botox because it makes me feel better about an imperfection on my face that I see. I don't need to explain or apologize about my choice to do Botox; it is not *selling out* or *being inauthentic* because that to me is being authentic to myself.

I have been partnering with Dr. Tracey Stokes, a fantastic plastic surgeon, for the past two years; to help her patients who are recovering from breast reconstruction surgery. My role is to tattoo their areolas back on to complete the journey of being cancer-free. It's something that I do to give back to women, and it makes me feel incredible. I wanted to partner with an all-female plastic surgery office because I think that there is a certain understanding and comfort working with women in this area of medical practice.

Dr. Stokes has also been monitoring my cyst for the past two years. I went in on June 22nd, 2018 to get a little Botox, and showed her a couple of pictures from my latest photo shoot. She measured my cyst again and said almost instantly, "It's time to take it out." OMG what? I wasn't prepared for that!

I responded, "What do you mean, 'It's time to take it out?' Really? Are you sure?"

Dr. Stokes measured it again and said, "It's growing, and we can't leave it in there any longer."

One week later on June 29th, I went into surgery and just like that, the benign neurofibroma was removed.

It's important to concentrate on what is right for you and not to look at other women and judge them for what they feel is right for their face, body or life. Everyone has their reasoning on why they choose to do specific procedures. Maybe you don't agree — you don't have to — but what you do need to do is support all women in a positive, uplifting manner. Don't tear down other women or be petty, catty, and hypercritical; we need more than ever for women to come together and lift each other up through the aging process.

I am sure you would like someone to wake you up when your hair is completely grown out and this gray hair journey is all over, but that is not how your incredible journey is going to play out. You are a strong, independent thinker; nothing is going to stop you, not even the dreaded *demarcation line!* So, let's talk about this, ladies; this "line" everyone is always talking about and trying to cover up.

OWN IT! Yes, own your gray *grow-out* and why not? Why are we trying so hard to cover everything up all the time? There is beauty in the *pretty little mess* of going gray. Believe me when I tell you, you will be so happy when you make it to the finish line. I am passionate about pushing you to the next level in your gray hair journey; where you decide it is the right choice for you, commit to it, and drive that gray home like a boss.

I want you to stop reading for a moment and list all the negative things that you think of when you think about going gray or allowing your natural hair to come out.

1. _____

2. _____

3. _____

4. _____

5. _____

Now I want you to take those negative words or statements that you wrote above and make them positive.

1. _____

2. _____

3. _____

4. _____

5. _____

This journey is about changing the way you think about aging. You need to write your own script and stick to it. Don't play by the world's rules; where is that going to get you? Looking like everyone else, that's where! Let your unique self come to life and flourish through this entire process. I am here with you, friend, *dig deep and find her!*

Write down your personal mission statement below. This is a great way to ground yourself in what you believe is true about yourself. Refer back to it when you are feeling low and on the verge of giving up.

_____

_____

_____

_____

_____

_____

_____

_____

_____

_____

_____

_____

SILVER SISTER SPOTLIGHT

MELANIE PEDERSEN

Hey, beauty industry hear us ROOOOAAARRRRR! That's right; next up is our beautiful Melanie, a thirty-nine-year-old retired Social Worker turned full-time wedding florist and part-time beauty YouTube guru. She is a mother to a precious six-year-old daughter, married to her best friend and loves all things beauty, specifically **makeup and skin care**.

Melanie, like most of us, is trying to figure out how to care for her new *gray hair* situation. Melanie started going gray in her mid-twenties and fought it for years until in her mid-thirties she decided to finally let go and embrace the new her by letting her gray grow out. She comes from a long line of strong German women who went gray very early in life. Both her Mother and Oma have the most beautiful silver hair; and they were her inspiration to finally give herself permission to "let it go." Melanie feels it was the best decision of her life and has not looked back. She loves the journey that she is on and is so excited to see so many Silver Sisters embracing their natural beauty when it comes to their hair.

Q: Tell us why you made such a powerful video titled "Why is My Hair Gray on Purpose?"

For the most part, the vast majority of my regular subscriber base was really supportive of my decision to let my hair transition. They were super encouraging. But others; not so much. I decided to make a video about why I chose to embrace my gray hair because while I received a lot of support, I was also constantly getting comments on my video from people as to why I would ever even consider letting my hair go gray. People told me I looked 20-30 years older than my actual age. It honestly got to be frustrating either deleting or constantly responding to these comments that were clearly aimed at making me feel like I was making the wrong decision. Comments like "You'd be so much prettier if you didn't have gray hair" really started to anger me.

My decision to go gray was based on a personal choice; I did not feel I needed to get permission from anyone. My gray hair actually made me feel 1000 times more confident and beautiful than my "fake blonde" hair ever did. My gray hair was me. I stopped fighting the inevitable and embraced a new version of me and I loved it. And the negativity from others surrounding that decision honestly just irritated me and I wanted to address people's "concerns."

Q. You decided to stop covering up your gray. How did that make you feel? Were you liberated or did you feel like it was a mistake?

I felt amazing once I finally decided to take the plunge. I guess I had a little confidence boost from the fact that so many younger girls were dyeing their hair gray at the time. I figured, no better time than now! I went to my hairdresser and we came up with a game plan to transition my blonde to gray. There was never a single ounce of regret. As soon as I saw my hair gray in the mirror, I knew I had made the right choice. I loved the way it looked! I knew it would take time to grow everything out, but I knew I could do it. Having the help of a talented hairdresser really made the transition much easier for me.

Q. As a mom with gray hair, how do you encourage your daughter to embrace her beauty and self-confidence?

I have always encouraged my daughter Stella to be herself. I have never imposed a certain beauty norm on her. She has always naturally gravitated towards being more of a girly girl. Her style is definitely feminine. As soon as she could choose her own outfits, I let her pick her clothing. She was under the age of 2 the first time she showed me a preference in the way she wanted to dress and how she wanted her hair. She didn't like pigtails or ponytails, so I never made her wear them. She liked accessories like necklaces and I let her style all her accessories by herself. She is always so proud of what she comes up with. While it doesn't always "match" it makes her happy and that is all I want. I also make sure she knows that beauty is more than just someone's outward appearance. Being beautiful on the inside by being a kind and caring person is far more important than any outfit or the lip-gloss you wear. I'm proud to say that my girl is one of the kindest more generous little kids I know. I'm so so proud of her!

Q. How has your personal style changed with gray hair?

Honestly, not a ton. I think considering the season of life I am in, being the mom to a super busy 6-year-old doesn't really allow me much focus on style. I am a classic soccer mom leggings/yoga pants and tunics kind of girl right now. Fashion is really not at the forefront of my mind at this point in time. I hope it gets to be again someday, but I'm ok with where I am at right now. It works for my job and my current lifestyle. My makeup has changed a bit. I do tend to gravitate towards cooler colors now that my hair is not blonde any longer. Warmer tones don't always look best so I have to be careful. But I will still rock a rusty brown eyeshadow if I feel like it!

I don't think your hair color should really dictate your personal style, necessarily. You may need to make some tweaks to feel like you look your best, but that is 100% up to you.

Q. What advice do you have for women just starting out in their gray hair journey?

My biggest piece of advice for someone starting out on their journey is to ignore the negativity that some people may throw your way. Don't let well-intended compliments like "You look so much better / younger

/ healthier with your blonde, brown, red hair" faze
you. If you think that NOW is the time for you to
start on your journey, then do it! And don't look
back, unless YOU want to. Do not let others dictate
your journey in life. If you want to be gray, be gray.
If you don't because you are just not personally
ready, then wait. But do it for you!

It's not necessarily easy to grow your hair out. While
a good hairdresser can get you started, it's a very
different reality to wake up in the morning and see
yourself with such a drastically different color. It can
feel like you are having to let go of something big.
But look at it as a new, exciting journey where you
get to be the new you. Wiser, bolder, more
adventurous. Embrace this new look and just **go for
it.** Just don't listen to others. No one has the right to
tell you how to rock your hair. That's up to you!

To connect with Melanie go to:

Instagram: @mrkongsmom
YouTube: MrKongsMom

SILVER LININGS

from this chapter

_____

_____

_____

_____

_____

_____

_____

_____

_____

_____

_____

_____

_____

_____

_____

_____

DRINK: OWN IT

1.5 oz Grey Goose Le Melon

3 oz Ginger Beer

3 oz lime wedges

Add Grey Goose Le Melon to a copper mug or highball glass and squeeze the fresh lime wedges.

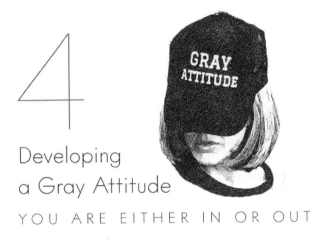

4

Developing
a Gray Attitude

"ATTITUDE IS EVERYTHING."

~Diane von Furstenberg~

LET'S KEEP IT REAL, GIRLS, going gray is very uncomfortable; at least for me, it was. I had black hair with white roots, and there is nothing cute and sexy about THAT. I wanted to try and see if I could speed up the whole "growing out" phase, but in reality, it just wasn't going to work. If I stripped my black hair, I was told it would turn orange, and I would be left with dry, brittle, lifeless hair.

Isn't this what we as women do with so many things? We find out it's going to be *uncomfortable* and try and determine how we can avoid at all costs being *uncomfortable*. What's wrong with being *uncomfortable?* Why all the panic? The phrase *"This too shall pass"* is a great motto to refer back to when you feel like your world is caving in all around you.

I decided that I would cut my long black hair down to a short chic French bob. I mean how can you go wrong with a classic bob? I loved it, and it felt so freeing; even though I didn't cut my hair to a pixie (I was one Pinterest picture away from doing a drastic cut).

There are many ways that women go through growing out their gray hair. There is no right or wrong answer it is a very personal choice, but in the end, you are either *In* or *Out,* but you can't be both. Cutting your hair is where your gray attitude is so important. You have to mentally prepare yourself for the transition you are going to go through. Commit to it and don't look back.

You might be thinking, *"That's great, Nikol; easy for you to say but this is so hard!"* It's only as hard as you make it. I have heard from so many women that they tried to lighten their hair, add highlights, or even strip all the color out so they could dye their entire head gray. I'm sorry to say that it just doesn't work that way ladies!

Stop trying to make this a fast process because it's everything but fast. The beauty is in *the process.* I want you to uncover all of the benefits that letting your hair go gray has in store for you. What would be the point of my book if you only read chapter one and skipped to the last chapter? Pointless, that's what! You would miss the meat of the book; the nucleus where all the secrets lie to uncovering how to be your personal best while going through a life-altering experience.

I designed a hat that says "Gray Attitude" on the front of it, and I have to be honest; the first couple of times I wore it, I felt exposed. I am not sure why; it was just so strange. I would forget that I was wearing this crazy hat then pass a man or woman on my walk and spend the next ten minutes thinking about what these random people would be thinking while looking at me. It was another hurdle for me to break out of this "shame" box.

Why did I care what people thought? I mean, I am
the one that put in big white letters on a black hat
GRAY ATTITUDE. I think it's because we all want to
be accepted and loved. When you go against the
grain you stand out, and you draw attention to
yourself, you are making a statement. Instead of
hiding behind my gray, I set out to create my new
gray attitude; even if that meant, I was
uncomfortable. Incidentally, I love wearing that hat
now! I wear it with pride and know I am making a
bold and powerful statement when I wear it.

Ladies, this is one of my most important chapters.
You must conceive it before you can receive it;
meaning, you need to *accept* your gray hair and the
new you before you can *receive* all the amazing
perks that come with being gray, silver, or white.

Remember the words that I mentioned in Chapter
One that we are using to define gray? Bold, Fierce,
Empowered, Authentic; that is what you are. You
need to believe it, see it, write it, and say it out loud
every day. I have interviewed so many vibrant
women that are going gray just like you for my blog
Beauty Reinvented. They are just like you and me,
navigating this crazy gray life and wanting to look
and feel their best.

SILVER SISTER SPOTLIGHT

SHELLEY MOORE

Our Silver Sister Spotlight in this chapter is on 'Dr.
Shelley,' a college professor who teaches
undergraduate and graduate students in the fields
of instructional design, adult learning, and
instructional technology at a large Midwestern
university in the U.S. She is married to her high
school sweetheart and best friend, who she met
when she was just 14. "We have two beautiful
children that I adore with all my heart, both
teenagers." Her latest hobby is training her first-

ever pup — a Goldendoodle named Ted — to become a therapy dog at the local Children's Hospital. "Just looking at Teddie makes people chuckle; I hope he can bring joy to the children and momentarily allow them to escape their illnesses." She also enjoys just about anything outdoors, including her butterfly garden, snorkeling in tropical waters, yoga, hiking, boating, and relaxing at the family's lakefront cottage.

I was so taken aback when I found Shelly on Instagram because her hair is so dramatic, fierce, and tells a story. It takes a strong woman to embrace her gray hair transition bravely. Shelly reminds me of a mix between an extraordinary woman that was in my life when I was a child, and Julia Roberts. When you look at Shelly's gray hair journey documented on Instagram, the beginning pictures have a lot of weight and uncertainty to them. As Shelly progresses, embraces, and allows her hair to almost develop like a butterfly, you can see the pure light that radiates within her. She is Bold, Fierce and Owning her beauty.

Ladies, this too will happen to you! I am so happy that Shelly agreed to be featured on *Beauty Reinvented*; her hair has a story to tell, and we can learn so much from her journey.

Q: At what age did you start seeing gray hair and what made you decide to ditch the dye?

I saw my first gray hair when I was 18 years old. Without blinking an eye, I bought a hair dye kit, and that was the beginning of three decades of dyeing. At that young age, it was already programmed in me that gray hair was something to hide. We must change this mindset. I found my daughter's first silver hair last month. I have encouraged her to think about not coloring her hair, should more silvers appear. Let's encourage our beautiful daughters to love their whole selves; to be confident in who they are, not in who society tells them they should be.

Q: You have a very powerful transformation. How did you feel when you started seeing the white roots?

I was admittedly horrified. Society has deeply entrenched us to think that silver hair on women is unattractive, yet men are more distinguished with their gray hair. It is ingrained in women that gray hair is 'old, ugly, shameful and that we should go to great lengths to hide it.' I have made significant strides in my evolution of how I perceive hair color. I now see the white, silver, brown, and steely gray as unique; and now that I am 11 months into my journey, I see a complete picture of what the end will look like and I cannot wait! There is no one else in this world that has my unique blend of natural highlights and lowlights. I am 100% unique now! No more hiding, no more shame. It feels so good just to accept it and move on.

Q: Did you find that society was shocked by your decision to be authentic with your hair color?

I was really worked up about what people would think, but the truth is, people truly do not care about other people's hair. Most ignore it. Some are confused. Some think it is intentionally dyed to look this way. One man said, "Wow, you must have paid a fortune for that hair color!" I have heard a couple of ignorant comments. But what I love most is when I catch another woman glancing at the new hair growing out of my head because when she smiles back at me, I am 100% certain I have encountered another Silver Sister in the making, and I hope I have given her pause to consider accepting her silvers.

Q: What do people say to you about your hair?

*I have had more compliments in the past year than I have ever had in my entire life put together! One woman chased me down in a furniture store to tell me how gorgeous she thought my hair was, and she ended it with "And I'm a **hair stylist so I should*** *know!" Random women and men have stopped me to tell me they like my hair. I stand out now. I am different than any other woman I know in my age bracket. I am a Silver Sister who has broken that bloody awful cycle of dyeing my hair and feeling the need to dye my hair every week because of the white halo that emerged about five days after every dye. What kind of quality of life is that? Every seven days I was embarrassed to go out because my roots were visible and it looked awful. I have had a humiliating year at times with a really awful demarcation line, but it was worth the trade because I am free now, and empowered. I am no longer held down. I have a greater quality of life, and I have so much more time to enjoy my life because I have broken this vicious dye cycle. I lived for the dye. It dictated my life. It was like a drug that I needed a hit off of to make me feel good. I am coming up on my "Silver Anniversary" — the one-year mark of having a healthier body and mind since ditching the dye. I am so happy to be in this place.*

Q: You have mentioned in your Instagram posts that your body became very ill from the toxic dye. Can you tell us what symptoms you had?

My body started to systemically reject hair dye in ways one would never directly correlate with hair dye; and now that I no longer dye, my symptoms have almost all disappeared. It started with digestive symptoms and food intolerances a few years ago and then moved to eczema of the eye. Every time I colored my hair, my scalp burned for days. After my last professional salon dye 14 months ago, my scalp was so damaged that every time I brushed my hair, electrical shocks were sent to my eye. Within 24 hours of my last home dye on May 6, 2017, my body went into anaphylactic shock, and for days I carried an Epi-pen with me, even sleeping with it, I was so fearful. I could not eat anything without my body reacting; my body was red, swollen and itchy; my scalp was on fire; my heart raced for weeks every time I ingested any food or drink. I honestly thought that my hair was going to kill me. My body was outraged, and it finally drew a line in the sand. Enough was enough. (And no thank you to all who have recommended the natural, organic hair dyes. I'm done!)

Our skin is our biggest organ, and when you make it absorb the toxic chemical frequently found in darker hair dyes, Paraphenylenediamine (PPD), it can have a dangerous impact. I fear the damage I have done to my body with dyeing my hair so regularly, and for so long, as it has been linked to cancer (American Cancer Society, 2018). Educate yourselves before starting or continuing on this journey. There are options!

Q: How have you dealt with the anxiety and self-doubt that gray hair brings?

I do **believe that "gray anxiety" exists** and it can be depressing, debilitating, and frightening for some. We have started a gray revolution because we want to empower women to embrace who they are, to reform beauty standards, and to learn to accept and love themselves as they are. I think many women mourn their youth so ditching the dye in a way, becomes symbolic of accepting we are growing older, that we are not immortal. And similar to mourning, I think there are stages we must work through on our journeys — shock, sadness, depression, and eventually, acceptance.

After recognizing that "shaming" my hair in front of my kids was only perpetuating societal views on **going gray,** I refrained from speaking negatively about my hair ever again. I relied heavily on my biggest supporter, my husband, who tells me every day how beautiful he thinks I am. I decided to be openly gray this time and never used the temporary hair colors to diffuse the demarcation line; for me, it made going public even harder after hiding and then revealing the hair again.

I also found great strength in the Silver Sisters who are part of my Instagram family. They are the most evolved, loving, compassionate, and supportive women. They are a close-knit group; they accept you when you fail, shower you with love when you need it, inspire you with their confidence; and humble you with their honesty and vulnerability. Many of the Silver Sisters are professional models, who are showing the world it's okay to age; it's okay to be gray.

-Connect with Dr. Shelley on Instagram @ Silvertransitions.

You don't need permission by anyone to go gray; you only need to give yourself that permission. Life is about experiences, not rushing through and missing out on all the unbelievable women you will connect with through your gray hair journey, meaningful connections, personal development and your newfound attitude.

I remember when I decided that I wasn't going to ask anyone for permission back in 2011. I was single at the time and had the honor of being asked by a magazine to be featured as one of South Florida's Finest Singles. I wasn't sure what to expect when I arrived to the shoot. At the time, I only had the gray stripe running down my head which the entire world loved to tell me looked like Cruella Deville (can I tell you how annoying this got?).

First I went into hair and makeup, then wardrobe. I was told I would be doing a "cover try" which meant they were thinking of me for the cover of the magazine. I got on set and the editor came up to me and said, "Um you wouldn't mind if we photo shopped your gray hair, would you?" I was so taken aback; so many things started to come to mind. *What? Is my little gray stripe not hot and sexy? Why would you want to cover up who I am? Single and gray, is that weird? I think if you are showing I am single, you probably want to show the real me, right?*

Do you see how an editor was trying to control how I looked to the public because of her limited views on age? She clearly felt that the gray was a *negative* aspect to my beauty. That was when I decided that no one will *ever* tell me to cover up anything about who I am or what I stand for.

Take my experience as a lesson and never let someone dull your silver strands or say negative things to you about your gorgeous authentic hair. You say to the world what your gray hair means to you; not the other way around.

SILVER LININGS

from this chapter

_____

_____

_____

_____

_____

_____

_____

_____

_____

DRINK: SILVER-TINI

2 oz Prosecco (chilled)

1 oz St Germain

2 oz Club Soda

Lemon peel to garnish

Pour all ingredients into glass.

Garnish with lemon peel; serve with ice if desired.

My 5
Strategies
to Going Gray

"GRAY HAIR IS A CROWN OF LIFE."
~Lailah Gifty Akita~

HOW ARE YOU DOING SO FAR? Do you feel empowered, bold, rocking a new attitude? Ready to take on your journey? I hope so because now is where the work gets good!

I feel that I can set goals if I have an outline on how I am going to get from *point A* to *point B*. I don't necessarily wing it, because when going gray you need to have a blueprint all mapped out in your mind on how you are going to get to the finish line.

Challenge: You are starting to see more and more gray tired of fighting with the toxic dye and ready to embrace what nature as in store for you.

STRATEGY 1: CHOP CHOP

If I have said it once I have said it a million times; cut your hair, ladies. I know that it's not necessary for everyone, but this is one of my best strategies to kick-starting your gray hair journey. You can't hold on to the dead hair with dye; it's just not what your new gray attitude would want you to do! Let go and embrace a new cut, look, and approach. Your outlook is compelling and is almost like a quick start to getting to the finish line. On average it takes two years to grow out your gray, so why hold yourself back with the same haircut you have had for the last ten years or maybe even twenty years?

It's fresh and liberating to cut your hair, and it grows back. I never thought I would keep the bob haircut when I first decided to go gray. I loved my long-layered hair; I knew how to work it with the round brush, I could get rock star blowouts, and flip my hair like no one's business. However, I was now forty and wanted to develop my style with gray hair. I thought, *once it all grows out I will let it grow back to what I am used to,* but I got so many compliments on my hair that I felt that I had more of a style with a shorter cut. Why have long gray hair that I end up putting up in a ponytail?

Some apps will show you what you will look like with different hairstyles. You can also peruse incredible Pinterest boards for inspiration. Create a board on Pinterest with hairstyles you love, ones you don't, and styles that are a little outside of your comfort zone. Show all of these hairstyles to your stylist. Getting a clear vision of what you want to achieve will make your transformation so much easier.

Your gray hair journey is a beautiful time where you will step out of your little hair box. Book that hair appointment and gain a new lease on your style. You need to feel confident about your decision to cut your hair; after all, this is a very personal decision and not one for your friend, husband, mother or partner to agree on for you. Be **bold** with your choice and **fierce** with your new cut. Believe me when I tell you, you will be *so happy* you took the leap of faith!

A note about hair stylists: Whether you have been with your stylist for a decade or you are searching for a new one, remember you will not necessarily get the support you are looking for from a stylist. Many women email me and tell me how nasty their stylist has been to them about not dyeing their hair. Not all, but a lot of stylists will not support this movement. Seek out a stylist that helps you and encourages you to let your natural hair shine. I have personally heard so many times how "old" I would look to "You are too young to go gray." Enough with all the gatekeepers; it is time to take your beauty and redefine it on your terms.

STRATEGY 2: CREATE YOUR VISION

I don't need to tell you how powerful visualization is to create your new life or the life you want to be living now. Vision boards are so incredibly creative! I have been designing them since 1998. I would have this ritual on every New Year's Eve where I would do a whole detox beauty routine, take a bath, drink champagne, and create my vision board for the upcoming year. As you can see, I wasn't a big New Year's Eve girl, but what I *was* big into was creating and designing the things that I wanted in my life. I wanted to see what my life in the New Year would look like all put together on paper.

Pinterest is a great way to make a virtual vision board. You can add to it or create a couple of vision boards at the same time, depending on how you like to work. I put my vision board right where I can see it each morning when I wake up. I want to keep my eyes on what I desire in my life and refocus if I get overwhelmed with being busy. I cut out pictures of women that inspire me, my favorite designers from Oscar de la Renta to chic French women showing how laid-back classic style is attainable. I cut out bold words and empowering quotes. I even put a picture of myself right in the middle of all my dreams. I put as many pictures as I possibly can on this board. I make it colorful, extremely personal, and exciting. It's my chance to dream big and design my life the way I want it to play out.

To create your own vision boards here are some supplies to make it easy.

1. *Poster board any size*
2. *Magazines (fashion, style, travel, beauty, special interests)*
3. *Scissors*
4. *Tape (I like the rolling scrapbooking tape)*
5. *Your favorite playlist*
6. *Champagne or any beverage that makes you feel glam*
7. *A great attitude full of dreaming big*

When you finish your vision board, take time to sit with your work, look at it, study what you just created, and meditate on your desires. Start your mornings with a cup of coffee and your vision board; play your favorite music and get into the zone. I have even gone as far as printing out little pictures or empowering quotes from my phone on my *Prynt* machine and sticking them in my agenda. I always have my life dream visions right in front of me.

Reach out to the silver women on social media that you connect with and that are going through a similar journey as you are. I started a private Facebook group for *Beauty Reinvented* because I wanted a safe place for like-minded women that were going through beauty struggles to come together and pick each other up. We have over 1200 women in this group that share freely, encourage, support each other, and post pictures of their gray hair progress. It makes me so happy to log on and see all the excitement and positivity.

Strategy 3: What Do You Need More Of?

The best way to keep yourself going and not obsess about all the change with your beauty is to get involved in your favorite activities. Maybe you love playing tennis but haven't because of work, kids or time? Now is the time to make that special time for yourself and do what you love. We are filled with joy and excitement when we do something we are passionate about, and that sets our soul on fire. Have you always wanted to take that baking class or painting class? What about that decadent wine-tasting workshop? Then do it! Go out there and start filling your calendar with things that make you feel *good*. Gray hair will have you on some days feeling like you just aged ten years when in reality it's just a little altering of color.

When I had days of feeling like I was crazy for letting my hair go gray, I would whip my hair back into a low ponytail or grab a hat and sunglasses. I would concentrate on planning trips with my husband, what wines we were going to try, what hotels were we going to stay in, and keep my focus on positive events. I would book lunch dates with my girlfriends or write out my editorial schedule for my YouTube channel to connect with all of you girls. I looked forward, not back; and with each six-week haircut, I was one inch closer to my goal.

How do you feel about your choice to go gray right this very minute? Write down how you are feeling.

_____

_____

_____

_____

_____

Are you ready to give up? If so, how does that make you feel?

_____

_____

_____

_____

_____

Write down you biggest challenge right now when it comes to your hair.

_____

_____

_____

_____

_____

What are you going to do about this challenge?

_____

_____

_____

_____

_____

STRATEGY 4: FACE THE FEAR

Fear is only allowed to fester if you give it the OK. We all have fears; there is no way to escape fear no matter how hard you try, but you can control it and have a healthy relationship with it. Are you afraid of going gray because of what people will think? Or do you worry what you will think about yourself? Will it make you older? Will it hold you back from advancing in your career? Gray hair will only set you back if that is the way you look at it.

What are your fears on gray hair right now? Write it down below:

_____

_____

_____

_____

_____

"WRITE DOWN EVERYTHING YOU FEAR IN LIFE. BURN IT.
POUR HERBAL OIL WITH A SWEET SCENT ON THE ASHES."
~Yoko Ono~

_____

Where are those fears coming from? YOU, that's right, and you can change them at any moment to a positive perspective on going gray, aging, and accepting yourself. The work comes from within. It takes time and patience to build your confidence and your positive self-talk, so don't be hard on yourself when you feel like you are being negative and can't get out of your rut. I knew I could either fear the gray or I could embrace my hair changing and be grateful. I guess I figured I had too many life fears already, so I wasn't able to add gray to the list. It wasn't overnight that my insecurity and anxiety went away, but my attitude stayed strong. On the days where my concern and self-loathing started creeping in, I would recognize it and move past that feeling, instead of letting the fear and negative emotions stay with me.

I was on a Reality Show in Hawaii in 2003. The production put together a little exercise for all of us to do to let go of the past. They set up a bonfire and had us gather around it. I carried so much emotional baggage from high school! The sad thing is, I was still dragging this baggage with me when I was on this show some ten years after high school.

The exercise had us reach deep

into the past to find material things such as pictures or clothing that held negative emotions and write down why they were holding us back. I picked my senior year football jersey that represented the emotionally toxic relationship I had with my high school boyfriend as well as everything school represented to me; all the secrets, hurt, and insecurities. We said out loud to the group why we picked such materials, and then we were to toss the items into the fire. It sounds stupid, but watching something burn that held so much emotion and pain for me was so liberating. You can do this on a similar scale by writing down all the negative experiences, situations, people, and so on that keep you from growing. Get out your shredder or find some scissors and cut up the paper into a million pieces.

"FEAR IS A GOOD THING. RUNNING AWAY FROM IT IS NOT."
~Kate Winslet~

STRATEGY 5: KNOW WHAT TO EXPECT

Let me preface this now; you will never know exactly what to expect, but you should prepare for all the pitfalls that go along with letting your natural hair color shine through. I didn't have any guidance when I went gray, so I want to make sure you know what to expect when you toss the dye.

You might think that your hair grows fast, but you will find out otherwise when you stop dying your hair. You will have gray roots, obviously, but you will also have a very visible demarcation line. Don't freak out

— we all have to go through this — but knowing what to expect before it happens makes it just a little easier. I had snow-white roots, a white stripe, and long jet-black hair; with one incredibly visible demarcation line. I chose to accept the two-tone color. I knew this phase wouldn't last forever and I wanted to get through it; not try and speed up the process by dyeing, bleaching, or stripping my hair. Too many women go down this rabbit hole and quickly find out that they have just made their hair situation worse.

By coloring your hair to ease you out of the uncomfortable *growing out* state, you create not one but three different colors in your hair when you start trying to speed the process up. Don't give in to the temptation to do this! Some women feel like this technique has helped them ease into going completely gray, but the majority of women feel like it is a huge mistake.

Play around with hairstyles that make your demarcation line softer; maybe part your hair differently or get creative with scarves, headbands, and hats. The first six months are the hardest, and your hair will tempt you every day to color it, but if I can do it, so can you!

Write Post-It notes all over your bathroom with positive words and positive quotes from women. Focus on your result; not the two-toned hair that feels like a science experiment. I know you think I am crazy, but you will look back at this time and see how much you have grown personally. Believe in your power!

"IT NEVER OCCURRED TO ME TO BE LIKE 'OH, NOW MY HAIR IS GRAY. I HAD BETTER ADAPT TO THAT.'"
~Linda Rodin~

Journaling is very cathartic, and I highly recommend you start writing how you feel about yourself, your journey, negative feelings, and positive comments. Write it all out, get it on paper, and release it to the universe. Writing is a time where you will be digging deep into the woman you are, and the woman you want to be. Be free, practice self-love, and if you can't think of anything to write that's OK. Grab a cup of tea or glass of wine, relax, and come back to it. Take your time to break away from the world and express yourself, to let out all of your feelings and insecurities.

I look back at what I wrote and feel so much gratitude for my journey because it was a journey of self-discovery, a unique and valuable time in my life that doesn't happen twice.

"A LOT OF PEOPLE ARE AFRAID TO SAY WHAT THEY WANT. THAT'S WHY THEY DON'T GET WHAT THEY WANT."
~Madonna~

Not everyone will think you are doing the right thing by choosing to let your gray hair shine but expect to start loving your gray, silver or white hair. Each day you will see progress. Keep looking at your vision board for inspiration, and consider a new haircut on your next visit to your stylist. Gray hair is a new world for you — get excited because it is just the beginning!

SILVER SISTER SPOTLIGHT

HILLARY BITAR

Hillary is a native New Yorker who went to the Fashion Institute of Technology. After graduating from F.I.T., she was a senior buyer at Bergdorf Goodman for over ten years. Hillary modeled for a short period as a teenager but was told she didn't have the right "All American" look. Fast forward to her adult life; Hillary married an Ambassador to Cuba, Belgium, and Uruguay which led to being overseas until 2009 when she moved to Miami.

Hilary reentered the modeling world at age 50. She went to an audition for a Zumba dancer and not only booked it but was used for all advertising of the Zumba Gold program. From there she was encouraged to pursue agents etc., and she did. Hillary is represented worldwide, and has worked almost five years as a full-time model. She has several TV commercials running at the moment along with ads for fitness, health, and beauty. Hillary says she loves the creativity of this business, but you also need to deal with an enormous amount of rejection- something people often don't realize.

Q: Tell us when you first started seeing gray hair.

A: I first started seeing my gray hair as early as my mid-20's! My hair was naturally very dark, so they stood out. I loved it and thought it looked like strands of tinsel. I never thought about covering them up. By the time I turned 40, I was indeed salt and pepper.

Q: What made you decide to go gray?

A: I decided to keep my gray because I loved being unique and I think it appealed to my rebellious side. With each negative comment I received (and there were many) it only made me more determined to stay true to my personal choice — not what the beauty industry and society dictated.

Going gray is not for the timid–it is a bold statement. Twenty years ago the internet was new, and there wasn't an online gray hair support community or chat groups – no info about the process, products to use, etc. Now it is so much easier and beautiful to connect worldwide with like-minded women "The Silver Sisters."

Q: You are a busy working model how has your gray hair enhanced your career?

A: My hair is my signature along with a 100% natural look. That's the image I chose as my brand. As a model, it has been both an asset and hindrance. The concept of accepting gray hair is becoming something other than "old lady/grandma," but the reality is that advertising is still youth-oriented. Women always search for any way to look younger and ads will continue to be marketed towards that. It happens often that a client will choose a woman my age with dyed hair over gray for that very reason. There is a fallacy about "dyed hair equals youth," and "gray hair equals old." But it is slowly changing and I am proud to be one of the pioneers.

Q: What has been your most exciting booking as a gray hair model?

A: Being chosen as the first mature gray-haired model in the Athleta catalog in 2016 was thrilling! I was featured alongside young women of all body types and ethnicities – I was truly proud to represent my generation.

I also had my first magazine cover in 2017 – M Magasin Sweden. The images are unedited and marketed to women over forty.

Q: What advice do you have for women wanting to go gray?

A: My advice is to go for it!! You will never regret it. Surround yourself with people (online virtual and real) who support You being You. Gray hair does inspire comments from virtual strangers that no other color will — so be prepared. Many are very kind and genuine — enjoy those and learn to ignore the rest which inevitably come from other women being cruel just because of their insecurities. Gray hair will make you stand out — Own it. Confidence is the key.

Connect with Hillary: Instagram @silverstorm

SILVER LININGS

from this chapter

DRINK: #DONTCARE

1 can of lychee fruit

2 oz Grey Goose

3 oz Lychee liqueur

Splash of lime juice

2 lychee's for garnish

Add a splash of champagne

Pour can of lychee fruit into a strainer. Reserve 2 tablespoons lychee juice. In a shaker, add crushed ice, lychee liqueur, vodka, lime juice and reserved lychee juice.

Shake well, then pour mixture into chilled martini glasses over a few pieces of lychee fruit from can. Add a splash of champagne and serve.

Xoxo-ing the
Negative Comments

I ALMOST WANT TO LAUGH WHEN I THINK OF ALL the negative comments I have received, whether to my face or on social media. You must know this comes with the territory of being a bold and independent woman. There is no escaping the harsh comments, but there is a way to deal with them. It is called

CANCEL

DELETE

So simple, right? Not exactly, but you must remember that all of these negative comments are not descriptive of you, but a reflection of the person that they are coming from.

In 2014, my husband and I went to Chicago for a little summer getaway. We were walking down Michigan Avenue, and a man (a little creepy) was walking towards us. He completely freaked out about my hair and said it *scared* him in this bizarre voice. You can image all day I said to my husband, "Do you think my hair scared him? ~*enter eye roll~*.

You have to have a sense of humor with all the negative comments that might come your way. Hey, maybe you will never hear one nasty comment about your decision to go gray, but from what I have experienced and all of the women I have interviewed, this would be wishful thinking.

"HATE. IT HAS CAUSED A LOT OF PROBLEMS IN THIS WORLD BUT HAS NOT SOLVED ONE YET."
~Maya Angelou~

Know that hurtful, nasty, and downright offensive comments might be a part of your journey, and that's OK. It's what you do with these comments that is important. I used to get very discouraged seeing nasty comments from women on my YouTube channel. It seems so unbelievably wrong that a woman would want to bring down another woman when I have built my channel on the basis of helping and supporting women through navigating their true beauty. I realized I couldn't control the comments but what I can control is how much space I allow them to take up in my mind; and that, my sisters, is ZERO!

Building up your self-confidence will allow negative comments to flow through your day without you holding onto them. They are hurtful and unnecessary, but the world we live in seems to feel it's OK to bring women down or try and make themselves feel better by saying not so nice things about your appearance.

Think of a negative comment another woman has said to you and write it down here:

Now let's reframe this statement. Rewrite this comment to be positive. If that's not possible, write what you would have liked this person to say. Now write something about this person that complements them.

_____

_____

Creating *positive energy* is the key to diffusing the negativity. For the most part, my thoughts would either make or break my confidence. I had to work on saying positive things to myself about how I looked on a daily basis. There were times when I would be watching TV, and a commercial would come on for a hair product, and I would see a woman my age jumping up and down in slow motion; her dyed brunette hair bouncing full of life. I would think *ugh...that used to be me.* I would snap myself back to reality and say THIS is WHO I am now. I can't keep looking at what I was. Living in the past holds you back. Ladies, we are moving forward into a better space both mentally and physically.

I started sharing and highlighting the negative comments on my Instagram stories and then made a video called "The Ugly Truth about YouTube and Social Media." I wanted women to see what kind of comments I was receiving and to promote women encouraging women.

We have a whole movement on women empowerment but where is that movement? Do you see it in your everyday living? Do you encourage other women? Do you go out of your way to lift another woman up? Think about that for a minute. I am not talking about getting involved in some massive march; I am talking about sending a card to another woman that is going through a hard time or congratulating her on an accomplishment with flowers or a little something. Taking the time out of your busy schedule to have coffee and listen to her without judgment, or simply talking with her. Inspiration and encouragement is what women need.

So much negativity surrounds us women about our aging, and we all seem too busy to care what's going on with one another. Check in with your neighbor, buy the woman behind you at Starbucks a coffee; pay it forward with a smile and caring heart. That's where the power is, ladies, it's within you and me. *You* determine if you are going to listen to the negative comments, and it is *you* that will decide if you fold and let other people's opinions about your beauty change your direction. It's *you* and only *you*.

Let's take it back old school and identify something negative someone said to you when you were young, and you accepted it as being real. You have held onto this statement throughout your life. For example, I was told in second grade that I wasn't smart enough to understand math. I accepted this as truth and struggled through math until high school. I believed this was true because a teacher — a respected adult — told me it was. I think back on that day and see how I allowed it to impact my confidence or lack thereof. In high school, I finally stopped believing this false belief but look how much time I spent not being my best self.

"YOU WILL EVOLVE PAST CERTAIN PEOPLE. LET YOURSELF."
~Mandy Hale~

Where in your life do you have false beliefs? What is holding you back? Do you feel like you keep doing the same thing, stumbling on the same rock in the road?

It is time to reframe your thoughts and beliefs about your beauty!

This chapter is not just about negative things people say to you: it's about the negative stuff YOU say to yourself on a continuous basis. I want you to *embrace* your aging with love and acceptance. Allow yourself to live without continually telling yourself why you can't do this or that.

I have had to do a lot of self-work coming from a modeling background where every day a client, photographer, or an agent would tell me why I wasn't good enough, didn't have the "right" look, was too short, hips were too big, or I wasn't tall enough or had the wrong hair color. I felt throughout my teenage years that I was dealing with all the negativity pretty well by looking at all I accomplished — being signed by FORD Models, spending my spring breaks in Eileen Ford's New York City apartment going on *"go-sees"* to Glamour magazine and Seventeen Magazine.

That time of my life was completely fascinating but I always had those negative comments swirling around in my head. They affected my self-confidence, my relationships, and my outlook on life. It wasn't until I was twenty-three and on a job in Jamaica that I decided *enough was enough* with all the negativity. I started to feel insecure, and I didn't like the feeling. I was constantly judged on my appearance, and I knew I had more than my looks to offer the world. So I took a break from modeling — my first departure from the fashion world in over ten years.

I went back to school to be a medical Esthetician and felt I had found my calling. I wanted to be more than my height, "Look," and sample size, so I did. I designed a life for myself that was built on the strength of my dreams and the force of my will because I told myself *I could do it.* I was smart enough and I was bold enough. I was *enough* and so are you.

What are you saying to yourself now that is holding you back from your true beauty?

_____

_____

_____

_____

_____

_____

_____

_____

What are your real life desires?

_____

_____

_____

_____

_____

_____

_____

_____

_____

_____

Write down your three biggest challenges when it comes to your beauty:

1. _____

2. _____

3. _____

SILVER SISTER SPOTLIGHT

BETH DJALALI — STYLE AT A CERTAIN AGE

Beth gives you solid, approachable fashion advice on her YouTube channel and total style eye candy on her Instagram feed. I love how she incorporates her classic style into everything she does from her Friday drink recipes to her Instagram stories.

Q: What age did you decide to let your hair go gray?

When I turned fifty, my stylist in Minneapolis suggested that the highlights we foiled in every three months or so were replicating my natural hair color. When she said let's go "au naturel," I said yes, and never looked back.

Q: How did you find your niche in the fashion blogging world?

Well, I always call myself the accidental blogger as I found my way into the blogosphere through a book I wrote but didn't get published. I did snag an agent who emphasized the importance of a social media presence for writers/authors. It took me two years before the light bulb went on to share my daily outfits through a blog and corresponding social channels. The twenty-year-olds were doing it; why not a fifty-six-year-old? Who knew it would be so much fun?!

Q: You have lived all over the WORLD; do you feel that living overseas has influenced your personal style?

Not having the opportunity to shop my favorite brands helped me to become creative with the items already hanging in my closet. When I came back to the States for a yearly visit, I learned to power shop a skill that serves me well as a style blogger. On the plus side, I had access to some amazing tailors and affordable tailor-made clothes while living in Asia. That was a game-changer!

Q: What are the three must-have fashion pieces every woman over forty should own?

Blazer, blue jeans, and a fabulous handbag.

Q: What wardrobe colors work best for women with gray hair?

Oh gosh, that's a hard question as I don't feel as if I wear outfits based on colors. Don't get me wrong; I knew there are certain colors that suit my coloring better than other colors. But I love brown and still wear it. I guess you'd say I like coloring outside the lines.

Q: What makes you "tick" when it comes to fashion?

I am a classic style girl through and through and have been since my teens. But I've learned to keep my classic outfits looking fresh and modern instead of stodgy and stale with accessories. Scarves, shoes, belts, handbags, and jewelry that are tied to the trends help!

Connect with Beth:

Instagram: @styleatacertainage
YouTube: Beth Djalali

SILVER LININGS

from this chapter

DRINK: EXPRESS-YO-SELF MARTINI

1.5 oz Grey Goose Vodka

¾ oz Kahlua coffee liqueur

¼ oz white crème de cacao

1 oz espresso (cold)

Pour all ingredients into a cocktail shaker, shake well, and strain into a chilled martini glass

Let Go
of Society's Perception

"WHEN THE WHOLE WORLD IS SILENT,
EVEN ONE VOICE BECOMES POWERFUL."
~Malala Yousafzai~

ACCORDING TO A DIMITRIUS DATA ASSESSMENT, "Women with gray hair are considered slow, not full of life, and old." This was written in a 2015 article on Today.com. The article continues to say that those who sport non-traditional hair colors can come across as *rebellious.*

Is pink hair *rebellious?* Maybe some view it like that, but I think going gray is the ultimate in being rebellious and I know that a lot of you feel the same way! You are making a statement loud and clear to the world that *you* don't need to *conform to dated thinking about age and beauty.* You are making your mark on the world on your terms. You are embracing freedom from toxic dye and gaining a new perspective on your natural beauty.

It's silly to say that we don't care what people think of us because we all know that's not true. To start moving the needle when it comes to reinventing what gray hair means, then we have to go full force ahead and not give a damn what people, society, or the gardener think of our naturally gorgeous gray, silver, or white hair.

What movement are you leading? Are media, magazines, or commercials influencing you to believe that you must dye your hair? Or are you feeling peer pressure because all of your friends are still dyeing their hair? Are you saying that you won't look good with gray hair? *Gotcha! I hear you sister, loud and clear!* How do you know unless you go for it? Remember, you can always dye your hair if you don't feel like it's the right move for you.

Gray hair needs a better PR team, and you have just joined this team. With more and more women from their twenties to nineties showing up bold, fierce, and ready to stomp on all of society's limited thinking, the more women will feel safe allowing their silver to shine.

I find it interesting that I was signed by FORD Models in New York City and Miami, went on to be represented by Elite in Chicago; Models One in Athens, Greece, worked the runway for Tommy Hilfiger with Rebecca Romjin, and became a member of Screen Actors Guild after auditioning a million times for union work. However, once I went gray, I said goodbye to my modeling career. I was represented by Elite Miami for a hot second in 2016 until they told me I was too New York, needed a tan, and was too sophisticated. It seems so ridiculous to me that I could have a career with fake dyed hair but with my silver natural hair no way. Why?

My conclusion is that people are afraid of aging and are stuck in this plastic box of ageless misconceptions. What's ironic about not being desirable or marketable to the modeling agencies I used to be with is that I have since settled several infringement cases with companies that have stolen my gray hair photos and plastered my face everywhere!

You have to get to a point where you stand up for yourself and your bold decisions. I spent way too many years walking into my agency being told how I needed to lose weight. It got to be such a drag because, being a size 2-4, I didn't know what they wanted from me. I was lucky that all of this pressure didn't cause an eating disorder, but I was one of the lucky ones. It was such an unhealthy environment to be continuously told why you are *not good enough;* not to mention looking at the model board with all the girls you competed with that either had the "perfect face" or "perfect body" or both.

Even though I went through the pressures of the fashion world, my life as a model wasn't a terrible experience. I was able to travel the world, be exposed to many cultures, interesting people, and exotic food. I met and worked with celebrities, got invited to the best parties, and worked with incredibly talented photographers and directors. However, I was controlled by the business. I had to be what they considered *beautiful* and that literally changed by the minute. I was allowing society's perception of beauty to dictate *my* opinion of my beauty.

It's not just society's pressure to keep dyeing your hair; it's everything from getting married by a certain age, having children, or being told you can't break the glass ceiling. It's all of this, and until you get fed up with ingesting it on a daily basis, nothing will change for you.

Take a good look at what you believe. Are those your beliefs or are they the beliefs society has imposed on you? There is a double standard for aging men and women. When are women going to stand up and speak out about this? How many articles do you need to read that glorify George Clooney and Anderson Cooper with gray hair?

Society celebrates these men, and in return, women are left holding the dye box!

Bold, Fierce, Empowered, Authentic describes women that are going gray. Everyone is aging and yes, it's a personal decision on how you embrace your physical aging. The more women that embrace aging, the more society will take notice.

I had a hard time when I turned thirty dealing with the pressure that society puts on women regarding marriage and having babies. I was a regional sales manager and trainer for a prestigious French skin care company, working like an obsessive beauty junkie to push the boundaries on my territory. I was on a plane multiple times a week living the exciting life of beauty and travel. One day, I was at a bridal shower and the soon-to-be bride's Mother-in-law, a well-spoken woman from the South, said to me in her pristine southern accent, "Nikol, what are you doing now?"

I replied, "Well, I am working hard, traveling and building my business."

She took a long look at me with a deep sigh and said: "Well honey, you are going to miss your time."

That one statement stuck with me for years. I allowed this ridiculous belief of hers to haunt me at every birthday, and subsequently to make poor choices based on her stereotypical comment. Why did I need to be married at a certain age? Have children at a particular time of society's choosing? Or choose not to have children after infertility? Why all the pressure? Until you draw a line in the sand between you and society, you will allow the comments and pressures to seep into your soul as I did.

Nora Ephron, an author and screenwriter, once said: "There's a reason why 40, 50 and 60 don't look the way they used to, and it's because of hair dye. In the 1950's only 7% of American women dyed their hair.

Today there are parts of Manhattan and L.A. where there are no grey-haired women at all."

Fitting into this "Youthful stereotype" is not realistic. Digging deep within yourself and finding the self-confidence and the determination to be who you really are is what is ageless. How do you do this? How do you get out from under society's blueprint for your life? You make a plan and stick to it no matter what.

When I was allowing my gray stripe to come out to the world at thirty-four, I went back and forth dyeing it. I allowed the pressure *to conform* get to me. I felt like letting the gray streak out made me look ridiculous because I was allowing society's view of gray hair to alter my decisions. Eventually, I made a commitment to keep my stripe and when my gray hair asked to be more than just the stripe I welcomed my new look.

Not every day will you feel like you've got society beat. There will be days that you want to retreat, drive back to the salon, or walk into the drug store ready to go back to the old you. Crappy days are the time for you to reach deep down inside yourself and ask, why? Why are you letting your thoughts, people, magazines get to you and knock you off balance? Taking that break and thinking about what's motivating you to regress will give you more clarity.

"TAKE CHANCES, MAKE MISTAKES. THAT'S HOW YOU GROW. PAIN NOURISHES YOUR COURAGE. YOU HAVE TO FAIL IN ORDER TO PRACTICE BEING BRAVE."
~Mary Tyler Moore~

Don't put your self-worth in the hands of the world — show up on your terms! It's what you think about yourself that matters; don't ever forget that.

SILVER SISTER SPOTLIGHT

ELISA IN MONTREAL

I am so excited to feature Elisa, a 52-year-old Italian-Canadian woman. She is a college educated professional working in an administrative field with international companies where her ability to speak five languages gives her a cutting-edge advantage in the business world.

Q: What made you decide to go gray and how old were you?

I had such a fantastic and wonderful life from birth to 50. Fun, parties, traveling, living life like from a magazine or nowadays from Instagram. If Instagram were available in my youth, I would have been an IT girl. Always willing to take up challenges and just be everywhere at once with tons of laughter and just complete and utter happiness. And then I turned 50! And it hit me like a brick. I WAS NO LONGER YOUNG. And I spiraled into a depression that lasted a full year, if not more. During this depression, I had gone to color my white hair roots, and while I was looking at myself in the salon mirror with sagging skin, etc. I said to myself "really? Like really? What are you? Who are you fooling? Stop it now and start accepting that you are no longer young." I was exactly 51.

Q: If you could change one perception of gray hair, what would it be?

My whole channel is about changing white hair perception Albeit all the great support I get from my fellow grey-haired ladies the rest of society is just not accepting it. Grey hair perceived by most is the end of the line. Period. I genuinely believe that only when the marketing machine starts working on making women with grey hair sexy, cherish-able, desired, valuable, vital, well everything they do for dyed hair but natural grey hair, only then can society be brainwashed to accept grey hair. Because on our own, it is never going to happen, love.

Q: You seem to have a funky style. Who and what inspires you?

LOL. For me funky style means crazy. If I look insane than all I can say is that I don't emulate anyone to look like this. I just take my risks while following proportion rules. However, when I see anyone anywhere with a particular outfit that attracts me, I will explore the possibility to interpret that look with what I have in my closet.

Q: How do you encourage other women to accept their gray?

I don't. I am not a white hair advocate. I couldn't care less how anyone looks as long as they are happy. I get many many many comments asking me if they should go grey. My response is always that going grey is not a hair issue at all. It's all about acceptance.

Q: Has your YouTube channel changed since going gray?

*I sincerely owe it all to **V from Grit and Glamour**. V had seen my first video on transitioning to grey, and because she followed my progress she gave my name a shout out in one of her videos, and I went from 160 subscribers to 1K within a month. Initially, I was not planning to do videos on my hair transition but instead focus on style. However, seeing the tremendous response I got from the first video, I just kept on doing development update videos. Still today they are the ones that generate the most traffic. I also changed with the transition. Whereas before my focus was on how to get a specific look, now my attention is on how to accept how we* *choose to expose ourselves to the world. The fastest and easiest way to happiness is acceptance of oneself and that of others.*

Connect with Elisa:

Instagram: @ElisaInMontreal
YouTube: Elisa In Montreal

SILVER LININGS

from this chapter

_____

_____

_____

_____

_____

_____

_____

_____

_____

_____

_____

_____

_____

_____

_____

DRINK: THE NEW BEAUTY

2 oz Grey Goose Vodka

.5 oz Fresh lemon juice

.5 oz Fresh lime juice

1 tsp. sugar

Drop of Crème de cassis

Rim a martini glass with crème de cassis and sugar

(first dip the rim in a shallow dish filled with crème de cassis and then into a dish of sugar)

Combine in a cocktail shaker with ice, strain into martini glass top with a drop of crème de cassis on top, and serve.

Reinventing Your Beauty – Makeup, Skin Care, Hair

8

THIS BOOK IS NOT ABOUT NOT USING FILTERS on your pictures or being told you can't explore Botox or Fillers. What I want for you to get out of this book is fierce, downright powerful self-confidence. Self-confidence that comes straight from your soul. I *know* you have it and I *know* you are ready to take the next step in reinventing your beauty.

Makeup shouldn't be complicated or intimating. Let's say you haven't taken the plunge and gone gray, but you feel out of touch with your makeup routine or skin care. Maybe you have little ones that take up all your time in the morning, or you have never worn makeup and want to give yourself a little refresh. In this chapter, I am going to share with you all of my easy and quick makeup tips.

For you ladies that are in transition or are entirely gray, I am going to tell you what colors are going to take your look to the next level. I truly believe if you look good, you feel better; and this is my number one goal for you.

What does *Reinventing your beauty* mean? We are all aging; there is no escaping the hands of time. As we age our skin changes and our coloring changes. Skin starts to feel dry; and pigmentation starts to pop up. Lines that were invisible on Monday are appearing on Friday. I have had one too many mornings where I looked in the mirror and did a double take. Wait! NOOO way was that spot there yesterday! Why do I grow hair on my chin, isn't this illegal?

Reinventing your beauty is accepting what you see in the mirror every day. It's telling yourself that you are *unique and beautiful* through all your changes. Don't just *say* it – *believe* it!

"IMPERFECTION IS BEAUTY, MADNESS IS GENIUS
AND IT'S BETTER TO BE ABSOLUTELY RIDICULOUS THAN
ABSOLUTELY BORING."
~Marilyn Monroe~

SKIN CARE

Let's start with creating flawless skin. Skin care is one of the most critical steps to updating your makeup look.

I see a real problem with women buying too many skin care products and then getting overwhelmed. You don't need ten products; I am starting with the basics to get you on the right path.

As a licensed Esthetician, I never wanted to overwhelm my skin care clients coming out of a facial. I would recommend the non-negotiables which were no more than two to three products.

1. Cleanser
2. Exfoliant
3. Moisturizer

Keeping it simple, basic, and focusing on real results is my goal for each client. Are you using dozens of products on your skin? Do you find you get overwhelmed with how many products you have? Here are my top, minimal recommendations for each skin type to allow you to hit the refresh button and be on your way to glowy skin.

A little side note: Ladies, you have to be patient and consistent to see results.

Dry Skin – Creamy cleanser, rice exfoliant, hydrating cream mask, moisturizer with SPF.

Normal Skin – Salicylic cleanser, either a physical or chemical exfoliant, clay mask, moisturizer with SPF.

Combination Skin – Glycolic or Salicylic acid cleanser, AHA exfoliating pads, clay mask, oil-free moisturizer with SPF.

Oily Skin – Glycolic cleanser, mild exfoliant (you don't want to over sensitize the skin) Spot treatment such as EradiKate by Kate Somerville, Retinol Drops (Rodial skin care) oil free moisturizer, face mask formulated for acne/oily skin.

Think of your skin as a garden. You need to water your garden to grow beautiful flowers, and the same goes for your skin. You need to feed your skin to get great results. For example, if you don't wash your face at night and leave on the day's makeup, dirt, pollution, and sweat, it's not possible to get glowing and youthful looking skin.

My Number 1 tip when talking about skin is to wash your face – it's like wanting to get an incredible body, but you don't want to work out. Once you get into the routine of washing your face every night, you will wonder how you even went to bed without doing this beauty ritual.

Next, you need to exfoliate two to three times a week. As we age, skin cells don't turn over as fast as they did when we were in our teens and early twenties. Removing the dead skin cells will not only give you beautifully buffed skin, but your serums and moisturizers will penetrate your epidermis and feed your skin. You are wasting money and product if you don't exfoliate your skin, because all those expensive serums, masks, and moisturizers will sit on top of all the dead skin cells and provide little benefit.

You can do this step easily by using EVER Skin Care "Reveal" pads or Dr. Dennis Gross MD Skin Care daily exfoliating pads. Exfoliating is a 2-3-minute game changer.

No one looks young and vibrant with dry, dehydrated skin — NO ONE. Moisturizing morning and night is a must. If you are already following this simple three-step skin care routine, you can power boost your regimen by adding in serums, peptides, and masks. Again, the goal is to feed your skin.

SPF is non-negotiable, but I want you to pay attention to your core routine first. Most day moisturizers and foundations include an SPF. If yours does not add sun protection, make sure you are applying a SPF 30 or higher before you use your makeup; even on cloudy days or days when you are inside.

Must Have's: Cleanser, Exfoliant, Eye cream, moisturizer with SPF 30+

As we age you have to start using AHA's, BHA's, physical exfoliants, Retinols, Serums, Masks, Eye Cream.

The difference between a physical and a chemical exfoliate are as follows: A chemical exfoliant is an acid like glycolic or salicylic that is breaking down and dissolving the skin cells. When you use a physical exfoliant, you are using a scrub that has little granules like jojoba beads that help to sluff off the dead skin cells resulting in smoother more youthful skin.

My favorite Skin Care and Makeup products to use include the following:

1. Kate Somerville-DermaQuench Liquid Lift

2. Korres Wild Rose Vitamin C Active Brightening Oil

3. Sunday Riley Auto-Correct eye cream

4. Sunday Riley Good Genes Latic Acid Serum

5. Beautybio GloPRO Microneedling Regeneration Tool

6. Natura Bisse Essential Shock Intense Mask

7. Ever Skin Care Canvas Priming Moisturizer Broad Spectrum SPF 30

8. Le Volume De Chanel Mascara

9. Patchology FlashPatch Under Eye Patches

10. GrandeBrow Brow Enhancing Serum

11. GrandeLash MD Lash Enhancing Serum

How are you feeling? Do you feel like you can get into a simple skin care routine with these tips? OK great; let's move on.

MAKEUP

Now that you have a pretty good idea how to cleanse, exfoliate, moisturize, and protect your skin it's time to talk about *Reinventing your makeup*. I understand that not every woman wants to wear makeup or navigate the crazy world of beauty. How many of you have gone to Sephora only to leave exhausted and utterly shocked at how many brands and choices are out there? Believe it or not, I feel the same way when I go to Sephora!

Here is a little tip on how to walk into Sephora and leave with just what you need. First, figure out what makeup you are comfortable wearing. Maybe you love mascara, but you don't like wearing foundation? Go into the store with that one objective and only buy the best mascara. On the next visit figure out what your must-haves are for that trip: a dewy foundation? Smokey eye palette or a hydrating lip balm? Write it down, focus on your makeup goals, and feel more in control when you leave the store.

Find out what you feel comfortable wearing. Maybe you love a tinted foundation but don't enjoy wearing a bold lip, or you love a full coverage foundation but like to keep your blush to a minimum. Figure out what you feel beautiful wearing and find the best products in that category. For example, I feel very comfortable on a daily basis wearing a natural eyeshadow palette – I experimented with a bunch of different palettes and finally created "Bottled Blonde" which received an overwhelming response from you when I wore it on my Instagram feed and YouTube channel.

Don't feel like you have to go outside of your comfort zone with makeup. *Less is more* as we age.

"HAPPY GIRLS ARE THE PRETTIEST."

~Audrey Hepburn~

Going from jet-black to silver hair has changed my makeup palette. Colors I once wore like browns dull out my eyes and don't give that "pop" of color that I need being on the cooler side of the color wheel.

Gray hair calls for brighter colors such as pinks, reds, corals, purples.

I never really wore a bright lipstick when I was a brunette, but now with gray hair it's what really makes my face look alive and gives me that extra bit of confidence. I love wearing my red matte lipstick called *"Secret Weapon"* or throwing on a glossy pink lip. When you have silver, gray, or white hair, you have to experiment with what you feel looks good with your hair color and skin tones. The colors I mentioned above are just a guideline to follow. Every woman will feel different in bright or muted colors; that's the beauty of makeup.

I talked about cutting your hair and updating your look in an earlier chapter, and the same goes for your makeup. What worked for you in high school or college most probably won't work for you now. I am not talking about your favorite mascara; I am talking about the thick eyeliner you wore or the outdated eyeshadow that's adding years to your face. I am here to be the friend that tells you NO! No, that doesn't enhance your beauty. It's time to change up your makeup. Reinventing your makeup will give you that fresh, feminine, and modern look.

You don't have to make your new gray hair makeup routine complicated. Let's keep it simple and concentrate on these four main areas of your face that make a huge difference between looking washed out or appearing on point, healthy, and pulled together.

Eyebrows are the key to looking young. Focus on your eyebrows — I can't stress this enough. Brow shaping and waxing to perfection are one of my specialties at Fresh Beauty Studio. Eyebrows frame your face, and if your eyebrows are sparse, light, spotty or too thin, they will make you look washed out. Defining your eyebrows with a soft taupe or brown pencil will add dimension to your face. You will be amazed at how eyebrows, when shaped correctly for your bone structure, can take years off your face. It's almost like a non-surgical facelift. There is power in creating the perfect eyebrow to complement your unique look.

I noticed when my hair went white in the front, I did not have a lot of color in my face. I know I have light skin, but this was ridiculous. I looked so washed out and not vibrant. Don't shy away from blush; make it your new BFF. I learned a great makeup trick when I worked as a freelance makeup artist for Bobbi Brown. Find where your cheekbone is — you can feel it with your fingers. Apply your blush on your actual cheekbone. Don't put it on the apples of your cheeks because once you stop smiling, the blush will bring your face down. As we age, we want everything to look sculpted and lifted. We don't want to look droopy.

Embracing a bold lip is a perfect way to take your look from zero to one hundred in a matter of a minute. I did a video on lipstick colors that were not right for me now that I have gray hair. I applied lipstick shades that were the wrong colors like brown, beige, and nude. Then I showed you lipstick colors that were right for me in the pink shades, reds, and corals. The right lipsticks perked up my skin and gave my face a beautiful overall look. Berry colors, pink-peach colors, and even a pinky-nude look gorgeous on gray haired women. Experiment and decide what makes you feel incredible, and then make that lipstick shade your signature color.

You can see I have a theme for gray-haired ladies when it comes to your makeup. You want everything to POP and to enhance your features. Don't let your eyes get lost by not lining them. Now the trick here is to find a soft shade like a chocolate brown, deep purple, or navy, depending on your eye color. I love using chocolate brown instead of black. It gives me just enough definition without the heaviness of black eyeliner, especially for daytime.

The key is to create a soft, natural, but enhanced look to your eyes.

Another great way to find the perfect makeup palette now that you are moving into the more mature and a gray area of beauty is to know what your skin undertone is which will either be cool or warm. Knowing your undertone will be a huge benefit to you when you start looking to build your new gray hair makeup collection. You will know what colors to avoid and what colors will make your skin radiant.

Some experts tell you to look at your veins to see if you have blue or green veins. Blue-toned veins equal cool; if you see green tones that tends to be warm. I am not a big fan of doing it this way. I like holding up a top that's warm or cool and seeing how it looks against my skin. You don't necessarily have to change your entire makeup palette. Look in the mirror and ask yourself how do you feel? How do you think the colors you picked look on your skin? Ask a trusted friend if the makeup colors you are wearing look good on you and give you life.

HAIR CARE

Now the section you all have been waiting for – HAIR. How the heck do you manage gray hair? How do you make it look gorgeous, soft, and not frizzy; did someone say out of control? Finding the perfect hair care routine has been hit or miss for me. At first, I gravitated toward products that were made specifically for gray hair, only to be disappointed with the results. I found when I concentrated on my scalp health with products from *Phyto* and used the *Ultime* collection from *Kerastase*, that my hair started to look hydrated and manageable, not to mention it smelled amazing. The key is to find products that don't include drying ingredients like alcohol.

My biggest advice is to treat and take care of your scalp for optimum hair growth. Scalp health comes in extra handy when you want your hair to grow as fast as possible during the dreaded growing out phase. Use shampoos that contain CoEnzyme Q10 that stimulate the generation of Keratin in the hair roots.

Gray hair tends to be on the dry side, so pay close attention to the ends by using conditioning moisturizers that include aloe vera, yogurt, wheat proteins, and panthenol. These will be beneficial, as they won't weigh the hair down.

Hair oil is another one of my favorites. Hair oils have come a long way with technology and are being packaged in spray bottle form now. Whether you have over-processed hair, split ends, or a dull look to your hair, rich oils made for your specific hair type will help build strength, luster, and suppleness to your hair.

Regardless if you are ready to dive in and go completely gray. We are all aging and our hair requires extra care. Don't forget that gray hair needs a UV protection to help keep your white super white. I found a great product to use on my hair years ago called *Micro-Voile Protecteur* by *Kerastase. Micro-Voile Protecteur* is a hair mist designed for natural and dry-to-dehydrated hair. It contains UV filters and reduces photodegradation. It is waterproof and has an anti-frizz effect on hair, which is a double win in my book.

The best cuts for mature women looking for a change with their haircut is chin or shoulder-length styles. A chic haircut such as a classic bob gives women a softer, more refined look. An excellent tip for thinning hair is to try a classic bob hairstyle with soft layers; this offers movement to your hair and makes hair appear fuller.

Cutting a little fringe or bangs are also a very flattering way to go when you are looking to update your hairstyle. Bangs can hide fine lines and wrinkles and give you a more youthful appearance. I love posting my faux bang look on Instagram, and I loved them so much I filmed a YouTube tutorial on how to wear faux bangs.

If you have long gray, white, or silver hair, creating extra volume with volumizing hair mousse or dry shampoo gives your look a boost. Try not to get stuck just pulling your hair back every day. I know it's tempting — I do it more than I would like to admit — but it's not a style, and it gets boring fast. Take time to work with your hair and get to know what your hair can and can't do. Let your hair represent you without you even having to say one word. Now that's powerful!

SILVER SISTER SPOTLIGHT

MARYAM REMIAS

Maryam lives in Los Angeles, California with her husband Eric and eight-year-old daughter Arianna. Maryam creates makeup, beauty and gray hair videos on YouTube and Instagram. Her favorite thing is to hang out with her family at the beach. She loves Persian food and Korean BBQ. It's safe to say she's a major foodie.

Before her YouTube career, Maryam had a corporate job working as a graphic designer. When she had her daughter she decided to stay home with her, but because of her workaholic nature, she needed to do something else besides being a stay-at-home mom.

At first, her hobby was collecting makeup and binge-watching YouTube videos. At the time Maryam was silently going through depression and was feeling very lonely, and YouTube was her escape. Her husband suggested she start her own YouTube channel rather than watching other people's videos. Creating beauty videos began as a hobby, but now has become an exciting career path for Maryam. The community of supportive women encourages her to keep going.

Q: Gray Hair is becoming a huge movement right now. When did you start embracing your gray?

I discovered a few strands of gray on the crown of my head at age 19. At that age, I related gray hair with being old. So, I refused to let anyone see my gray roots, and that's when hair color and I were inseparable.

Through my mid 20's, I had developed skin allergies to hair colors. I knew something was wrong with coloring my hair, but I wasn't ready to show my gray.

*It was in 2014 that I started to embrace my **gray hair journey**. What led to me embracing my grays was that I was tired of coloring my hair every two weeks and the skin allergy on my scalp had gotten terrible.*

I remember the day when I thought that growing out my gray hair could work for me. I had looked up gray hair on Pinterest and found beautiful older women with naturally gray hair. Also, pictures of young women with colored gray hair that looked fantastic. That's when I started to become curious about how I would look with gray hair.

I spoke to my husband and showed him the photos on Pinterest. He was supportive, and we both wanted to see how it would turn out. I'm very thankful that it became a trend because it gave me the courage to stop coloring my hair.

So, I started my transition journey and embracing my gray hair in 2014.

Q: You have a YouTube channel where you teach women about beauty and style. Did you feel insecure doing videos with gray hair?

I was insecure in the beginning about doing beauty videos as a 40-year-old woman with gray hair. It was scary to put myself out there and get out of my comfort zone. I was also going through so many ups and downs with transitioning to gray hair.

The only way I could deal with the emotions was to talk about my gray hair transition on video. I used my YouTube channel as a vehicle to tell my story and share my journey with others.

I figured by sharing my story I would help someone going through the same situation and hopefully make an impact in their life.

Q: How do you encourage other women to start their gray hair journey?

The way I encourage other women to start their gray hair journey is by sharing my story and sharing tips on how to get through their transition. I give the resources that helped me transition to gray hair. I also share the videos that I've made about gray hair on my YouTube channel.

Here are a couple of resources that I used on my journey.

• Looking up "Women with Gray Hair on Pinterest" — You'll find many beautiful women with gray hair with different skin tone and hairstyles.

• I also recommend joining Gray Hair Facebook groups — They are a very positive and an encouraging place for anyone going through the transition.

• Lauren from How Bourgeois was an inspiration to my journey to gray hair.

Going gray is not for everyone, and the only way you know for sure is to try it out. You may fall in love with your gray or silver hair and never think about coloring again.

Q: Do you feel that gray hair is a trend or a movement?

It was a trend for younger people to dye their hair gray but that trend seems to be going away.

In the past six months, I feel that there is a movement of natural gray hair. I've been seeing lots of women with gray hair on social media sharing their transition journey or just rocking their beautiful gray hair.

It became undeniable when a few months ago, Maye Musk became the new face of CoverGirl. I also knew that beauty industries view of women with gray hair was changing when beauty companies started to reach out to work with them.

Q: Social Media can be harsh at times with the negative comments. How do you handle negative comments about your gray hair?

It can be very harsh. I've gotten my fair share of negative comments on Instagram but very few on YouTube. What's weird is that I get negative comments from women close to my age, but the younger generation is more accepting.

I don't answer negative comments because the people writing them are looking for attention. I believe that the more focus you give the negativity, the more you receive it.

My hope is for everyone to embrace their uniqueness, no matter what their hair color, size or age. We all have a voice and story to tell, and we can all learn from each other.

Connect with Maryam Remias:

Instagram: @MaryamRemias
YouTube: MaryamRemias

SILVER LININGS

from this chapter

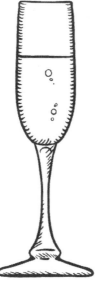

DRINK: EXPENSIVE CHAMPAGNE

Need I say more!?

9

Build Your
Silver Sister Club

"Spread love everywhere you go. Let no one ever
come to you without leaving happier."
~Mother Teresa~

It was through my connection with women
from my infertility journey that changed my life. I
can't imagine what my journey would have been like
if I didn't have the support of other women by my
side that were going through the same hell I was.
We all want to feel loved and to be accepted. Life
throws us a lot of curveballs, and it's up to us to
decide how we are going to move forward. Aging,
going gray, unexpected life experiences that you
never saw coming — I am right there with you, and
it's tough. That is why I am writing this book; for you
to know you are not alone with your struggles when
it comes to aging, gray hair, feeling out of place,
insecurity, and feeling like you lost yourself
somewhere along the line in the hustle and bustle of
life.

There are many days where I am bummed out about this or that. I spend way too much time thinking and worrying about things that will never happen. I start trying to control all aspects of my life, and then realize that I am the clay, not the potter. God is in control of every single second of my life and it's the challenge I face every day to understand that and to flow with my life; not resist it.

I am stronger and better because of you. You have helped me in ways you probably don't even know from your comments on my videos, emails, and messages across my social platforms. They genuinely have touched me and kept me going when I felt like giving up both on the fertility and on my gray hair journey.

I find myself thinking, *what would have happened if I never pushed myself to come out publicly about my infertility struggles?* I would never have made the connections around the world with women that felt the same way and who made me feel normal. *What would have happened if I thought I was too broken to do a YouTube video on my grey hair journey? Too worried about what the world would think of a woman in her thirties coming out about going gray?* Look at all the women that I would never have met!

Beauty Reinvented is a community of thousands of amazingly strong, fierce women in my private Facebook group. WOW, my life would be completely different if I didn't reach out and open the doors to connecting. I feel that it is critical to your success when deciding to go gray to reach out and join Facebook groups, start a blog, or leave comments on other accounts you admire that inspire you so you can begin creating a relationship with other women that are going through the same life challenges you are. We are here for each other to love, support and lift up.

There is nothing wrong with letting yourself feel sad, angry, or frustrated about what is going on in your life; the problem comes with how long you allow that time to occupy your mind.

"THERE COMES A TIME IN EVERY WOMAN'S LIFE WHEN THE ONLY THING THAT HELPS IS A GLASS OF CHAMPAGNE."
~Bette Davis~

Women are powerful, and together we can rule the world. I mean isn't that what Beyoncé preaches? Who Runs the World? GIRLS!!!! I believe it and so should you. We are one *powerful* group of women telling society that we are not going to take the stereotype of gray hair to mean *old* and *outdated* anymore. We are here together to encourage each other to live our best life whether we choose to dye our hair or let our silver run free.

Find like-minded women that share your same outlook on aging and going gray. Surround yourself with positive, uplifting people because you don't have time for low vibes when you are painting your world platinum.

SILVER SISTER SPOTLIGHT

VAHNI LEVITT

Vahni *(also known as V.)* is a gorgeous silver sister that not only has her Master's degree in professional writing, but also a YouTube channel and a glamorous Instagram feed. I met V. through YouTube, and we share not only our gray hair journey but the same Greek heritage.

V. is a first-generation Greek-American who is three months into her gray hair journey. She has spent the last two decades developing and publishing digital content. She is also the voice behind Grit & Glamour, a fashion and lifestyle blog that she began in 2006. V. has served as a panel moderator and panelist at Independent Fashion Blogger conferences, and has been featured in The Sydney Morning Herald, Grazia Magazine Australia, and on dozens of other blogs. V. calls the Southeast home, and loves entertaining and spending time with her Aussie husband and her dog Macy.

Q. Tell us why you decided to go gray.

I've been dyeing my hair since my late 20s. I used to get away with many weeks between touch ups, but as the years passed and my grey multiplied, the time between root touch ups got shorter and shorter. Finally at age 44 (after two failed attempts to grow out my grey the previous year), I decided enough was enough. I was tired of trying to time touch-ups around holidays, events, and vacations. I was tired of worrying about people seeing my grey roots...and using eyeshadow and mascara to hide the silvers two weeks after coloring. I was tired of knowing within four weeks, I'd HAVE to make time to color my hair. I was tired of my scalp being irritated by the dye. I felt like it was time to accept who I was under the dye, come what may.

Q. Who is the woman or women that inspire you in the gray beauty revolution?

The catalyst for my change in perception of grey hair is the model Kristen McMenamy. After modeling in the 1990s, she kind of disappeared for a while, then she showed up in Vogue in 2010 with this incredible, waist-length mane of silver hair. I was dumbfounded. And captivated. And I guess the seed was planted in my mind then.

Then when I saw U.K. Vogue editor Sarah Harris' never-been-dyed, natural white-grey a few years ago, I had the same feeling. These were women in fashion who chose to embrace their natural grey hair at a time, an age, and in an industry where this was definitely not the norm. They are mavericks. They made me feel like going grey in my 40s was a kind of rebellion (I've always been a little rebellious). It takes so much courage to choose to go grey at any age, but especially in your 30s and 40s. And it tells the world, "Hey, I'm not playing that game anymore. Here I am, like me or not." I started to see that being youthful and sexy has zero to do with your hair color and age. It all comes from within. It's how you carry yourself.

Kristen and Sarah definitely got the wheels turning in my mind. Then when my mother gave up being platinum blonde and grew out her stunning natural white hair, I was sold.

Q. Do you feel the beauty industry is embracing the gray movement?

I do. It has taken a ridiculously long time, but better late than never. I do see the tide changing, and I think we kind of have Millennials to thank for making dyed grey hair a thing. But I think perspectives on aging (and age, in general) have shifted significantly in the last 50 years. We are healthier, smarter, and more active than ever. So it makes sense that women like Carmen Dell'Orefice and Maye Musk are enjoying huge popularity well after traditional retirement age. I think the beauty industry is just starting to wake up and see that women at all ages are relevant.

It's about time we expanded our perspectives and product lines to accommodate the massive spectrum of ages, appearances, and ethnicities that exist today. I love Christie Brinkley, but in the 80s, even I felt the sting of being a freckled, brown-haired, hazel-eyed girl in a world of blonde, blue-eyed beauties. I'm elated that the beauty industry has made such incredible strides over the last several decades. There should be room for all of us at the table.

Q. What is your favorite hair product?

Man, I couldn't live without Living Proof's No Frizz Nourishing Styling Creme. My grey is a mixture smooth and wiry. The only thing that keeps me from looking really, really bad on humid days is the No Frizz. That and coconut oil. Absolute miracle stuff, it is, especially for longhaired ladies.

Q. How has your personal style changed because of going gray?

There are several colors I feel like I can no longer wear, and consequently, have had to let some beloved pieces go. Off white, rusts, browns, and beiges really don't look good with my cool salt-and-pepper roots. Since my hair is in transition (and will be for years to come), I have salt-and-pepper roots, and reddish-brown ends. I feel like patterns outside of stripes are a no-go, and I never wear more than two colors at a time. It's just too busy with my already busy-looking hair. I tend to stick to black, white, grey, pink, or cool-toned colors like blue and lilac. But really, it's just mostly black. Black was my default color, even before the grey.

In terms of style, I've always classified my style as sophisticated with an edge, and that still holds true. But I do maybe dress a little edgier or more rocker than before; I don't mind looking a little older because of my grey, but I do mind looking frumpy. Also, at nearly 46-years-old, I feel that it's important to invest in quality pieces...a good handbag, quality shoes. At this age, I don't think one gets away with wearing a lot of cheap things. When everything is lower quality, you project low quality. I don't mean to sound harsh. Obviously, people should wear whatever they want. But from my perspective, I've been working for 20 years in my career and I want my persona to project that. I want to look like I have my you-know-what together.

Connect with Vahni Levitt:

Blog: www.gritandglamour.com
Instagram: @Gritandglamour
Podcast: Grit and Glamour

SILVER LININGS

from this chapter

_____

_____

_____

_____

_____

_____

_____

_____

_____

_____

DRINK: PLATINUM-TINI

3 oz Grey Goose L'Orange

.5 oz Premium Orange Liqueur

1 splash white cranberry juice

1 squeeze lime

Shake all ingredients in a cocktail shaker filled with ice.

Strain into a martini cocktail glass

Serve with an orange peel

Creating
Your
Silver Lining

I HAVE TALKED ABOUT HOW GOING GRAY is not comfortable, and it takes a bold step in your journey to break out and say — Here I am — and I am OK with this.

Brave, Fierce, and in control is what you are; and I am so proud of you for making this decision or even thinking about going gray! But what if you find yourself thinking, *"Right... I read this book, and it seemed to be an easy journey for you, Nikol, but it is not so easy for everyone."* I think from what I shared with you in this book that you know this was not easy for me, but I decided to choose (key word there CHOOSE) to *embrace* this journey. I intentionally talked myself through the days where I wanted to feel safe and go back to dyeing my hair.

You have the power to create anything you want in your life. You determine if you are going to wake up and look in the mirror and love everything that is looking back at you. No one else will define your happiness. *You* hold the power! Speaking of power, why give it away to people that say negative comments or flash you a disapproving snarky look?

Determine before you start letting your gorgeous gray, silver, or white hair out that you don't have room for negative vibes — surround yourself with people that support you, lift you up, and encourage you through this process. If you find yourself struggling with finding the right kind of support, I would love for you to come over to my private Facebook group *Beauty Reinvented* for encouragement. What are you waiting for? All the ladies are ready to push you forward and be your sounding board.

Even with just my gray stripe, I experienced probably one of the worst encounters with a man that made me feel incredibly insecure and terrible about the beginning of my gray hair journey (last story I promise). I was on location for a bride in Harbour Island, Bahamas; working on creating gorgeous hair and makeup. After my stylist and I finished the wedding, we walked over to a nearby restaurant where we could hear the lyrics to Bob Marley's song *"No Women, No Cry"*, which would soon become the theme of the night.

We were sitting at the bar enjoying a much-deserved glass of wine when an older man stumbled up to me and said, "Did you know you have a genetic disease?" He caught me mid-sip of my crisp and fruity Sauvignon blanc.

I turned around on my bar stool. "Excuse me, what did you just say to me?"

He repeated it again; barely getting out the entire sentence, just of course, the keywords hair, genetic disease, you. He kept saying it over and over, and each time he got louder and louder. I was on the verge of a major meltdown — not only did I just deal with the pressure of making our bride look incredibly flawless (in the middle of an unusually hot December on a tiny island with a flash tropical storm practically ruining her hair and the beach wedding), but I had just flown back to Florida from Colorado from my last IVF #5 retrieval then jumped on a miniature prop plane to do this wedding! I was spent, both mentally and physically. I was a wreck waiting on the Pre-Genetic Screening results, feeling super bloated, heavy from all the synthetic hormones, and just not myself (heck I hadn't been myself in years due to all the fertility treatments, but what was new?)

It didn't matter that this inconsiderate lout was drunk, what mattered was that my self-esteem had just been put through the blender in a very public way. I turned to my stylist, and she could see tears well up in my eyes. "Does my gray stripe make me look like I have a medical condition?"

My friend took my hand and said, "Of course not, he's drunk and out of his mind!"

Together we watched as this jerk stumbled down the dock and into the darkness. I had a choice to make: Let this complete loser ruin my night; or upgrade my white wine to a Nik-tini and that's exactly what I did.

"I AM NOT AFRAID OF STORMS FOR I AM LEARNING
HOW TO SAIL MY SHIP."
~Louisa May Alcott~

I sincerely wish I had punched him in the face and then had some cool moves like Cameron Diez in Charlie's Angels — and whoops did you fall off the dock? Sorry, not sorry. Ladies, that was the hormones talking; he's beyond lucky that didn't happen because it really could have and I think the international police would have taken my side, given the number of hormones found in my bloodstream. Always pull the hormone card (unfortunately my husband doesn't fall for it anymore). I chose to create my silver lining from this experience.

Remember when I said in Chapter two to write down a feature on your face that you love? What was it? In my case, it's my smile. It's unbelievable how you can change your whole outlook by putting a smile on your face; even if you have to force it at first.

I woke up the next morning and stepped outside my beach cottage, looked at the glistening pink sand (what Harbour Island is known for) and listened to the waves crashing on the rocks. I closed my eyes, took a deep breath of salt-filled air, and counted my blessings. I am a powerful woman, determined and passionate. I am an entrepreneur that gets the privilege of being booked to do what she loves on this exclusive island and make women beautiful for their wedding day.

"CHOOSE YOUR THOUGHTS WISELY FOR THEY HOLD YOUR FUTURE."

~Nikol Johnson~

Create your game plan and stick to it. It's OK if you get derailed through this journey but come back to this book and get inspired to recharge your gray hair journey. You are worth it!

Take the time to write down five powerful adjectives that best describe your personality.

1. _____

2. _____

3. _____

4. _____

5. _____

Pick out one and write it on a post-it this week and put it on the front door so that every time you walk out you are reminded of the incredible woman you are. If you are having trouble, pick out adjectives of the woman you want to be.

Invest in yourself and your self-confidence, and you will not be disappointed.

I feel so honored that you picked up this book and have made it to the end with me. I can talk about Silver Linings and make analogies all day, but truth be told, *you* are the Silver Lining. All you have to do is be present, hone in on your unique beauty, and help other women with this aging process. I love the saying, "You are right where you are supposed to be at this very moment in time." Hold on to that saying when you feel weak.

Stop second-guessing yourself and asking everyone for permission and approval as to whether you should go gray. Why do their opinions matter? *You* are the one wearing the gray hair; this is for *you* to decide YES or NO!

Challenge yourself and everything you have thought in the past about gray, silver, and white hair. Take the time to put on lipstick or mascara and show up. Honor yourself and give yourself permission that YES, you can. I am here for you every step of the way cheering you on from my YouTube channel, Instagram, Private Facebook group, and blog.

I hope you have found this book helpful to ignite your inner Silver Storm and push you to the next level.

If you loved this book, I would be thrilled if you would write a review on Amazon and share it with other women that might be struggling with the gray hair transition.

Lastly, and as a personal favor to me, take a picture of yourself reading this book and post it on social media with the hashtag #BeautyReinventedBook.

I want to celebrate our community of powerful women leading the *Beauty Reinvented Revolution.*

Ladies, You Know What Time it Is — *It's Time to Get This Beauty Started.*

Until my next book *(or until I see you on Instagram, Facebook or YouTube).*

Nikol

GRATITUDE

I want to take this time to thank all the special people that encouraged me through this entire process of writing my book. It's no mistake that my experiences from infertility to my gray hair journey happened to me because God has had bigger plans for me than I ever could imagine. Like my Mother-in-law always says, "When God closes one door he opens another." To my husband – who has been there through the ups and downs of my hormones, white stripe, gray hair journey and all my crazy moments – thank you for always being there, loving me, putting up with me, and pushing me ever forward. I have taken your "Figure it out" to the next level.

To the incredibly fierce women that contributed to this book: Melanie, Hillary, Elisa, Maryam, Rhiannon, Shelley, Beth, and Vahni, thank you! Without your passion for gray hair and desire to push the boundaries, my blog and book would not be what they are today.

To my dear friend Karrie, that met with me for our "business dinners" over the years and listened to me through all my crazy book ideas: thank you for encouraging me and being my support team through this process.

To my parents and my best friends: thank you for support and unconditional love. You have been my backbone throughout my life, supporting me, laughing with me, crying with me, and most of all, allowing my creative spirit to soar.

And finally, to my readers: without your support, this book would be just a dream.

Printed in Great Britain
by Amazon